# Taking the Stage

## BY ALICIA ECONOMOS

D1528732

Copyright ©2020 Alicia Economos
All rights reserved.

ISBN: 9798625281126

••••••••••••

## DEDICATION

Dedicated to my Father God
and four of my most treasured gifts:
Ted, Kristin, John and Jessi

• • • • • • • • • •

# THE CAST OF CHARACTERS

Leading Female: *Alicia Economos*
Best Supporting Male: *Ted Economos*
Supporting Roles:
    *Daughter Kristin, son John, and daughter-in-law Jessi*
The Medical Team:
    *Dr. Tom Buroker, Dr. Tim Gutshall, Dr. Scott Hamling*
    *Dr. Bill Heggen, Shari Houston, Dr. Konstantinos Lekkas*
    *Dr. Jim Lovell , Dr. "Thor" Halfdanarson , Dr. James Andrews*
Featured star of the show:
    *Father God, Emmanuel (God is with us)*

• • • • • • • • • •

# THE CREW

A special thanks to the following people who helped get this publication finished and in your hands, listed in alphabetical order:

Julianne Bartlett
Kelly Bartlett
Nancy Bell
Diane Cutler
Kristin Economos
Denise Erhard
Tammy Kesler
Sue Luehring of SJL Design
Amy Nichols (Publishing Agent)

And a special thanks to all of my family and friends. I couldn't have done this without the support and encouragement from each one of you. I love you!

• • • • • • • • • • •

# THE ORCHESTRA

After working for nearly 20 years as a life coach, I've heard a wide variety of stories and I've learned something from each one. I've asked women to be vulnerable with me and the others in their coaching group for the purpose of making heartfelt, deep connections with themselves and with each other — and with God. This past year, I felt it was time for me to be vulnerable and pull the curtain back on my own story — the good, the bad, and the ugly.

Unfortunately, far too many little girls were raised in toxic, abusive households involving alcohol, drugs, or physical and sexual abuse, and that's heartbreaking. Helping those women process and get free from their past is one of the greatest joys of my work.

At the same time, the vast majority of my coaching clients came from what we'd think of as normal families. But "normal" is nothing more than a setting on a washing machine. Let's face it; we all grew up in Dysfunction Junction to some extent. It's just the *degree* of dysfunction that helps us to distinguish between families that are *more or less* healthy.

Although physical wounds are often more visible, emotional wounds can be equally damaging; nonetheless, we must avoid making comparisons, for regardless of the degree of our wounds, they're all relevant. If they're keeping you stuck and living half-heartedly they're important and deserve the attention to break free of them.

Throughout my upbringing, my family looked nearly perfect, *from the outside*. We had a beautiful home, nice cars, went on vacations, and had many of the nicest material things you could imagine. Had you asked me about my childhood, I'd have said, "It was good." However, when I reached adulthood my eyes were opened. I began to question the obstacles I repeatedly encountered and in doing so discovered some deep wounds that needed to be dealt with.

In retrospect, my life looked like a beautifully staged production. Yet behind the scenes was a much different story. People weren't prepared for the roles they were intended to play, and they'd failed to show up for rehearsals. Consequently, the performance was lackluster at best.

However, this is *not* a book about bashing my parents or anyone else. Instead, as I always tell my clients, we can assume that every parent got up each day and tried to do the best with what they knew at the time. Truly, nothing more could be expected from *any* parent. Therefore, we must extend grace and forgiveness to all parents.

*At the same time*, we must deal with our wounds. We're not to pick a side (either your parents or that little girl or boy within yourself), but rather, choose both: forgive parents and go back and process the hurts and unmet needs of your heart.

In the fall of 2010, God literally downloaded some simple tools that helped me to get free from my past. Eventually, those tools evolved into a decluttering program called Wholehearted Living. Decluttering means to get rid of the stuff (emotional, physical, and spiritual) that prevents us from living our best life. Over time the original download was further developed and became the core materials for our program; three, eight-week courses that involve weekly small group coaching sessions. Through the program women are able to process their past — regardless of their upbringing, embrace the present and be better equipped for their future.

At some point, each woman must define for herself what it means to live wholeheartedly; however, these three definitions seem to resonate with most women:

- To live wholeheartedly means to know who you are, know who you aren't, and be okay with both, and as a result, having the strength to show up with congruence between who you are on the inside and on the outside.
- To live wholeheartedly means to live with an inner peace, confidence, and joy despite even challenging circumstances.
- To live wholeheartedly means to love God, yourself, and others with *all* your heart. (Matthew 22:37-39)

Ultimately, my story is intended to help you develop a healthy relationship *with yourself*. Since that relationship is the most influential relationship you have, getting that one on solid footing will have a positive impact on *all* your other relationships — including your relationship with God.

In the First Act of this *production* you will hear stories about my upbringing, what I experienced and how those experiences impacted me. Keep in mind that events can *and often do* impact people in different ways. Therefore, this is only *my* perspective and how things influenced *me*. Although your upbringing may have been quite different, I believe you will resonate with my story and see that we all have more things in common than not.

The Second Act covers my spiritual or faith development. Then, in the Third and Fourth Acts, I present the steps to develop more satisfying relationships — both a healthy relationship with yourself and a vibrant relationship with God.

Finally, in the Encore you will see an assortment of articles that I wrote as my story progressed. The purpose for including them is to reinforce what you learn so you can master it. If you are committed to living wholeheartedly please keep the following in mind; massive repetition is the mother of success — whereas dabbling is the mother of frustration and failure.

---

**. . . massive repetition is the *mother* of success — whereas dabbling is the mother of frustration and failure.**

---

Many other women started like I did, believing they weren't good enough, smart enough, pretty enough, or in some other way not "enough." However, after completing the Wholehearted Living courses they were able to live with confidence from knowing and valuing who they really are; they learned to embrace the fact that they're a "piece of work" — meaning *both* a masterpiece and a work-in-progress, just like you and me.

How great would it feel to discover the incredible woman you're created to be? Although you might not have gotten acquainted with her yet, she is closer than you may think!

Let's dim the lights and get on with the show!

# ACT I

## *My Relationship with Myself*

· · · · · · · · · · ·

## SCENE 1: OUCH!

One day (as an adult) I was driving home from an event and was stopped at a nearby intersection. While I waited for the light to turn green, I thought to myself, "I need to remember to go straight so I can stop at the grocery store, rather than turning left and heading directly home."

I'd recently learned that the average person has over 35,000 self-thoughts per day, so as I waited a few minutes I probably had a dozen or more thoughts. So when the light turned green I did what was most familiar to me, which was to turn left. The moment I realized what I'd done, I silently yelled at myself, "You idiot! You have the attention span of a gnat! I just told you to go straight and you've already forgotten. What a loser!"

Did my self-talk seem a little harsh? *Absolutely*! The reality of my situation was that I could just take the very next right-hand turn, and I'd arrive in the same parking lot. No kidding!

The crazy thing is that if the same thing happened to one of my friends and I was riding along as a passenger, I'd never dream of talking like that to her! I'm guessing you wouldn't, either.

Instead, I'd be quick to offer grace and likely respond with something like, "Don't worry about it. You have a lot on your mind right now, and it's completely understandable how you'd forget. Plus, you can still take the next right turn and end up in the same spot, so it's not a problem."

Do you hear the remarkable difference between my two reactions? God's Word tells us to love our neighbors as ourselves, not instead of ourselves!

(Matthew 22:39) Like me, might you have grown comfortable loving your neighbor while being hostile to yourself?

---

### Like me, might you have grown comfortable loving your neighbor while being hostile to yourself?

---

Although this incident might not seem too significant, it certainly wasn't an isolated one. Any given day I could have come up with hundreds of other examples because, for as long as I could remember, I'd been my biggest enemy — and sadly, I had no idea how to be anything else.

I wondered if anyone else felt the way I did: exhausted, lonely, and discouraged from trying to be good enough. So I continued to try to hold it all together. But in reality, I felt like I was falling apart.

It happened over a long period of time, but I'd slowly developed a toxic relationship with myself. Yet had you asked me about the status of that relationship, I'd have laughed at you. I didn't even know I had a relationship with myself, or that there were tools that could help me to improve it.

You're probably not surprised to hear that the average woman is hard on herself, but the *percent* of her daily thoughts that are negative and self-defeating might surprise you. Research shows that over 75 percent of a woman's self-thoughts are harsh and critical. That's like mentally beating ourselves up three-fourths of the day, every day!

**IN THE SPOTLIGHT:** The following article of mine can help you see that we're not the only ones who suffer from an unhealthy relationship with ourselves:

#### What Do You Have in Common with Whitney Houston?

In 2012 we learned of the death of Whitney Houston. How unfortunate that someone who was so talented, beautiful, and faith-filled died at the age of just 48! Quite honestly, at first I didn't believe it. How could someone who seemed to have it all have lived such a tragic life?

Maybe you and I have more in common with Whitney than we could have imagined. Whitney had some problems that included failed relationships; addictions to drugs and alcohol; and apparently, the biggest problem of all, her unhealthy relationship with herself.

Many people were aware that Whitney got her start by singing in church. She appeared to have a strong background of faith. So how could someone who seemed to have a personal relationship with Jesus have missed out on the peace and contentment that He made available for each one of us?

In a previous interview with Diane Sawyer, Whitney was asked, "What is the number one 'devil' in your life?" Her response said it best: "That would be me. I'm either my best friend or my biggest enemy."

What about you? Are you your biggest fan or your biggest critic? How healthy is your relationship with yourself? What are your own thoughts like — especially those directed at yourself? Are they supportive, empowering, and encouraging, or harsh, critical, and condemning? You get to choose, and whether you're aware of it or not, with every thought you're actively choosing one or the other.

Our relationship with ourselves, starting with our thoughts, can be a major contributor to anxiety, stress, depression, sickness, and disease. Unfortunately, instead of dealing with the core issue, as a society today we often resort to medicating the symptoms. Rather than experiencing those unhealthy and sometimes catastrophic results, why not learn to go straight to the problem: your relationship with yourself? That's where genuine, lasting transformation always begins.

When interviewed about the death of Whitney, Barbara Streisand said it best: "How sad that her gifts that brought us such happiness couldn't do the same for herself."

The same could be said for most of us, unless we do some work.

Much like Whitney Houston, as adults we cause most of the pain and anguish in our lives. We routinely cause major heartaches and headaches — all that are completely avoidable.

We find ourselves feeling stuck, not for a lack of effort, yet feeling like the harder we try, the further behind we find ourselves. We fail to realize the root of our problem, and instead focus on changing the symptoms.

Some people suggest the answer is to feed ourselves a lot of positive thinking. Unfortunately, that'd be like putting gallons of water on a garden full of weeds. The truth is that even a truckload of positive, encouraging thoughts can't override a toxic and unhealthy relationship with yourself.

---

**. . . even a *truckload* of positive, encouraging thoughts can't override a toxic and unhealthy relationship with yourself.**

---

As I share about my own background, you'll see how easily we develop an unhealthy relationship with ourselves. And in later scenes, you'll learn how to turn that relationship around.

• • • • • • • • • • •

# SCENE 2: UNFINISHED BUSINESS

Like all parents, mine had some unfinished business from the previous generations. They married at a very young age, and neither one was equipped to develop and maintain a healthy marriage.

My mom was an only child and her parents were well-mannered, quiet, and very concerned about appearances. My dad had a younger brother, but their age difference was so big that it was as if he, too, was an only child. His parents, however, were hard working, jovial, *and loud* (and, I thought, very fun). Sadly, because they lived so far away, we only got to see them about once a year or even less.

When I was in junior high, we began to send handwritten letters to each other. Unbeknown to me, my grandfather saved every one of the letters I'd written. Decades later, he gave them to me bound in a three-ring notebook and, of course, in chronological order. He was the ultimate record keeper and had a system to organize everything!

Even though we rarely saw them, I have fond memories of visiting them in their home in Parkersburg, West Virginia. They had a dog — a

Dalmatian named Sunday and a horse named Rosie. Both were especially fun for my sister and me.

One of my favorite things about visiting them was spending time with my grandmother, whom we called Granny. She was full of life and made me feel extra special. She had a sense of humor, an infectious laugh, and made friends easily and effortlessly *anywhere* she went. Although I didn't see her very often, she still made quite an impression on me.

My grandfather, Bernie, had a more business-like approach to things, yet he'd always greet me with a big smile and deliver the same message in his booming voice. He'd give me a hug and whisper in my ear, "Alicia, I believe that girls are smarter than boys, so if you apply yourself, you can do anything you put your mind to!" How I wish both of my grandparents were still alive today so I could tell them how much I love them and what a tremendous impact they had on me.

Unfortunately, because of my parents' wounds from their upbringing, they both felt like they had something to prove. This generated a marriage and later a family of their own, with a lot of emphasis on appearance, performing, and gaining others' approval. What mattered most was how things looked on the *outside*, rather than what was going on *inside*. In addition, their generation wasn't inclined to see counselors, therapists or coaches, so their issues were just swept under the rug. Sadly, what was swept under the rug had a toxic stench and, eventually, it wafted my way.

It wasn't long before I learned that I wasn't perfect (not at all shocking, I know), but there was an expectation that I *should be*. That belief, plus several others, got an early start in my life. When I was just a year old, and my sister was almost four, my mom took the two of us to have a professional photograph taken. I was dressed in a frilly white dress with layers of crinoline. (In case you're not familiar with that, it's stiff and scratchy material that provides extra bulk or body to a skirt or bottom half of a dress). I have no idea how long we had to sit in such uncomfortable clothes while the photographer took the pictures, but photo shoots always take longer than young children want to sit still.

A few weeks later, the black-and-white photograph was framed and proudly displayed on the wall of our living room. Over the years friends and visitors would often comment on how cute the picture was. My mom's response was always the same (and I heard it far too often); she would say, "Well, thank you. Alicia couldn't sit still long enough so they had to give her a prop (a plastic flower) to get her to cooperate" — as if she was perturbed with me about my behavior.

Now I don't mean to throw my mom under the bus with this story, but at the same time that was the acorn that was planted and eventually became a thriving oak tree in my life; it was the beginning of the lies that I wasn't "good enough" *and* that I was "too much."

Through the years, with each repetition of that story (plus many other incidents) I began to believe that I *should* have been able to sit still for a long period of time. I became convinced that something must be gravely wrong with me, and that my energy and enthusiasm were problems that needed to be fixed.

There was one day in kindergarten that I remember as clear as if it were yesterday. My classmates and I were starting an art project that involved the use of paints. I was dressed in a freshly ironed yellow cotton dress, with a white peter pan collar and three little ducks along the hemline. (It was definitely a bit fancy for school, but my appearance and the clothes I wore were important to both my parents.)

As we started painting, I decided that instead of using the paintbrushes it might be fun to paint with my fingers. I no sooner stuck my finger in the bright blue paint than the teacher reprimanded me with a very stern voice *in front of everyone.* Then she made me put the paints away and sent me to sit quietly on my mat that was supposed to be just for naptime. I remember her loud complaints included the fact that I was in such a pretty dress I couldn't risk ruining it although, like the rest of the kids, I had on a painting smock that covered the entire front of my clothes.

That experience might seem incidental, but it was humiliating for me, and it left a painful impression; it reinforced the belief that I was "too much," and it eventually led me to shrink back and withhold my creativity.

• • • • • • • • • • •

# SCENE 3: THE DAMAGE OF SUGAR!

In my grade school years, my dad was often gone; he'd be working at the hospital (he was a surgeon), attending meetings, exercising, socializing, or doing something else away from our homelife. When he was home, he was usually preoccupied or seemingly irritated, and he often had a short fuse. I learned it was wise to stay out of his way, so I'd avoid being scolded for something. He often found fault with my words or behaviors, and so his moodiness seemed to be a reflection of his disappointment in me. I knew without a doubt that *in his eyes*, I didn't measure up.

My mom was technically a stay-at-home mom, but she did plenty of volunteering, especially for the animal rescue league. She and my dad both loved dogs so we had a Dachshund named Sugar, and later a yellow Labrador Retriever named Molly. I often wondered why my parents were more comfortable showing their affection to the dogs than they were to their kids — or to each other!

One afternoon my sister and I were sitting on the couch together with Sugar. She was fairly old and was a bit cranky — *the dog*, not my sister! She was sitting on my lap and was chewing a bone. (Can we agree that was a *very bad* idea?)

I was talking and (as usual) was fairly animated with my hand gestures. Apparently given my movement, Sugar thought I was going to take her bone, and so she bit me in the face! She left three puncture wounds in the middle of my cheek! It was scary, painful, and humiliating. The response of humiliation might seem a bit odd, but you see it reinforced that I was somehow damaged goods.

(When I share this story, people are often surprised that I didn't become fearful of dogs. Fortunately, I'm a dog lover, but I'm also very aware of keeping a safe distance from a dog's mouth, *especially* when they're chewing a bone or a treasured toy.)

Many years later, at my dad's suggestion, we went to see a colleague of his, a plastic surgeon. The doctor felt confident that with a surgical procedure, he could improve my facial scars from the dog-biting incident.

(Unfortunately, it did nothing to deal with the more devastating scars — my emotional ones.)

A few months after my surgery I overheard my parents talking about the results; my dad voiced his disappointment with them and needless to say, I felt even *more* self-conscious about my scars. For almost four decades, whenever I looked at myself in a mirror, those scars were the only thing I saw. Fortunately, the decluttering process freed me from being bothered by them. (It could also be partially due to the fact that gravity is doing its thing and wrinkles distract one's eyes from them!)

Among some of the challenges of my upbringing, there were also carefree days of fun with my sister Jennifer, who was almost three years older than me. As grade-school kids, we were often creative in our play; when Molly, our Labrador Retriever, was just a six-month old puppy, we attached her leash to the handle of our red wagon. We were so surprised that although we'd lined the sidewalk with a trail of her dog treats, she wasn't able to pull the wagon with the two of us sitting inside it (waiting for what we'd hoped would be a fast and fun ride).

I also remember Jennifer putting me on the handlebars of her bike and riding to the neighborhood grocery store. It was a fun outing, and we'd pick up a package of gum or occasionally an item Mom wanted us to bring home.

Some afternoons the two of us would take a blanket outside and sit on it under a shade tree in our side yard. I loved breathing in the fresh air and listening as she'd read one of the Nancy Drew mysteries out loud. I'd eventually lay down on the blanket and stare up at the sky, trying to find animals or objects in the puffy white clouds. If I close my eyes, I can almost smell the fresh breeze and still hear her voice sharing the adventure story with me.

Other times, on a summer evening after dinner, my mom would take us to the local Dairy Queen. Sometimes our dog Sugar would get to go with us, and we'd purchase a small vanilla ice cream cone *just for her*! (I think it's fair to say that we spoiled our dogs rotten and to this day, I do the same with my own dog.)

Despite the fact that neither of my parents provided a lot of what I needed emotionally and spiritually, they both had some great qualities that influenced me in positive ways. My mom had a great sense of humor, was a gifted writer, and was very talented musically. She also exposed me to her ability to sew, often making a dress for my sister or me for homecoming, prom, or some other special event.

One thing both my parents enjoyed was to open our home to guests. They'd often host lunches, dinner parties, tennis matches, and occasionally even themed parties; whether entertaining friends or work associates, they tended to every detail and made people feel comfortable.

Also, from my dad, I inherited energy and enthusiasm for life. He led by example, to take the lead and work hard — *very hard*. He also enjoyed exercising to stay fit and taking photographs; both were things I grew to enjoy and continued to make a priority in my own life. Also, he was a reputable surgeon and accomplished a great deal in his profession. It was just too bad that his success at work came at the expense of his homelife; his actions left collateral damage that negatively impacted us for decades.

Both my parents would often say, "Whatever you do, do it to the very best of your ability." They also said, "When bad things happen don't waste any time complaining about it, just get on down the road." The first saying promoted perfectionism, and the second one was a formula for stuffing your feelings and ignoring what happened. Unfortunately, those sayings were deeply ingrained in my head.

Throughout my grade-school years, although I was an average student, a very good reader, and a follower of rules, I continued to get the message that I was a problem. Every one of my report cards *(every quarter of every year)* indicated that I had a specific area that "needed improvement;" I needed to talk less. (If only I'd known then what I know now. I ended up becoming *paid* to talk as an author and speaker!)

• • • • • • • • • • • •

# SCENE 4: THE ROUGH WATERS OF JUNIOR HIGH

As I entered junior high I continued to feel like a misfit. We lived in a much nicer house than my friends (which was embarrassing), my parents were different than those of my friends, and I lived with the constant pressure of needing to be perfect. Despite the fact that we had many of the nicest things, these differences left me feeling odd, misunderstood, and lonely.

I was also very small for my age, so I had to shop in the little kids' section of the local department store, Robeson's. No surprise then that the clothes I had to choose from were *nothing* like what my friends and classmates wore.

I distinctly remember going to a junior high school dance where my good friend wore a "cool" pair of bell bottom jeans, a suede belt with fringe on it, and a psychedelic print shirt. I, on the other hand, wore a short, white knit dress with navy piping and three bright red stars across the chest. And to complete that "lovely ensemble," I wore blue and white striped knee socks with navy blue suede shoes! (Talk about standing out like a sore thumb!)

In addition, even though I'm now quite an extrovert, I was very unsure of myself and therefore, I seemed more like an introvert. Believing I wasn't as smart as my peers, knowing I didn't *look* like them, and struggling with other insecurities all contributed to feeling like I didn't belong.

In hindsight, I more than likely had A.D.D (Attention Deficit Disorder); but back then I had no idea what that was. I've since realized how much my need to move and my inability to focus for any lengthy period of time were telltale signs. (As an adult, I freely share that I've self-diagnosed myself with A.D.D. However, I've redefined that to mean, **a**dorably **d**elightfully **d**isorganized!)

When I was in seventh grade, I made the cheerleading squad. Tammy, Kenda, and several of my other good friends were also on the team, and we had *a lot* of fun. In a gymnastics class I learned how to do a back "flip-flop," which I got to do in our floor routines at half-time of the basketball games. I was also the one who had to be on the top of our pyramids, but I was afraid of heights; yet given my size, I didn't really have a choice.

That same year my mom took me to her hairdresser, Robert, to have my hair done. He gave me a perm, a *really curly perm*! When he was finished, I walked out of the salon looking a lot like a poodle! I could tell by the look on my mom's face that it *wasn't* a good look for me.

Of course as luck would have it, that was the week for our school pictures to be taken for the annual yearbook. I wanted to die! Nonetheless, I showed up with my brown and white large checked dress with a big collar piped with white rick-rack. (It was a stunning look for sure!) My hair was *so bad* that my mom agreed to take me back to the salon the following week and paid to have it straightened. Unfortunately, I didn't get to have my school picture retaken.

Our neighbors to the south of us, the Callahans, had a pool in their backyard. They'd allow us to come over anytime we wanted to, and because their daughter Kenda was one of my best friends, we spent a lot of time there. Another family, the Bells, who lived across the street and one house down from ours, also had a pool. They, too, made us feel as if *their* pool was *our* pool.

One day my dad decided we should have a tennis court in our backyard. (Swimming pools and a tennis court sounds like an ideal country club, right? *Trust me* it wasn't like that, *on so many levels*.) Although my mom played tennis, they'd not discussed the idea of adding a tennis court. As my mom retold the story, she said she'd had no clue until she looked out the kitchen window and saw a giant truck pulling into the driveway.

She called my dad at the office to find out what was going on, and he told her he'd decided to have a tennis court put in our backyard. That was apparently the first she knew of it! That type of incident wasn't unusual, given their poor communication with each other — and sadly, that lack of communication didn't improve.

• • • • • • • • • • •

## SCENE 5: HIGH SCHOOL AND SEPARATION

I attended Mahomet-Seymour High School, which was very small, and therefore, there were a limited number of extracurricular activities for girls; cheerleading and track were about our only options; however, we did have physical education classes that provided a variety of activities like dodgeball, scooter tag, square dancing, ballroom dancing, *and* volleyball.

As a freshman, I had P.E. classes with upperclassmen, and several were popular guys from the basketball team. I really wanted to impress them, but I was still peanut-sized and looked more like their grade-school sister.

In addition, I was afraid of the volleyball, so I tried to avoid it at all cost! Not surprisingly, I missed the ball far more often than I ever connected with it. Eventually, all in fun, the guys gave me the nickname, "weak spot" — not exactly a name you'd want engraved on a plaque. It only further cemented my belief that I didn't measure up.

Fortunately, I tried out for cheerleading and made the team every year. Again, Tammy, Kenda, and several other friends were also on the team, and it was great to be part of something that made me feel like I fit in. Yet at the same time, my appearance continued to be a source of major insecurity. I was skinny, short, and hadn't yet begun to develop. Being a late bloomer contributed to my feeling of somehow being "less than."

To make matters worse, of my core group of ten friends, seven of them were in the advanced math and science classes. That left just me and two other friends who were in the normal classes, which further cemented the belief that I wasn't smart enough.

At that time, my dad worked long days at the hospital, and my mom was often busy running errands, volunteering, doing housework, or absorbed in a sewing project. By this time my sister was off to college, so our house was fairly quiet *and lonely.*

I worked a limited number of hours as a cashier at the IGA, which was our local grocery store. I really liked my job *and* having my own spending money.

When I wasn't in school, working, or studying, I was often home, barricaded in my room by my own choice. I spent *hours* listening to albums, often setting them up all around the room, as if they were keeping me company as I sang along. (Surely I wasn't the only one who did that?)

When I was a senior in high school, despite my belief that I wasn't smart, I'd accrued enough credits so that I could finish my senior year while also attending a nearby junior college. I took two accounting classes and discovered that I actually enjoyed studying when it was a topic I was interested in. Even though I did well with those college-level classes, it didn't change my belief that I wasn't smart enough; that belief was too deeply ingrained in my head.

I remember a time when my dad asked me what I wanted to do for a career. I told him that I really liked accounting *and* dancing. He told me there wasn't likely a big demand for dancing accountants. (Funny thing is that I eventually found a way to incorporate both of my interests; I was a bookkeeper and office manager, and I also taught aerobic dance classes. Who says you can't be a little creative in pursuing your interests?)

That same year, my parents separated. One Saturday afternoon, without any warning, my mom and dad called me to come downstairs from my bedroom. They were standing in the foyer of our house, and my dad told me that he and my mom had been having some problems, and that he was going to move out. He had a suitcase already packed and waiting at the front door. He gave mom a big hug and a passionate kiss (which was *very* embarrassing *and* confusing to me), and then he walked out the door and drove out of the driveway.

I was shocked! It wasn't like I'd heard my parents fighting or yelling, because to my knowledge, they didn't do either one. Though in retrospect, our house was often quiet, and there was a lot of unspoken tension in the air. But at the time that was all I knew so it hadn't been too concerning — it was just lonely.

My mom surely must have asked me if I had any questions or wanted to talk, but the only thing I distinctly remember is that within ten minutes after my dad's departure she got out the vacuum cleaner *and started vacuuming!* Unfortunately, that was her way of coping.

My way of coping was to retreat to my bedroom where I was alone with nothing more than my thoughts and a lot of unanswered questions. I was understandably scared and sad and felt very much alone. I was also worried about what others would say about my parents being separated, and I couldn't help but feel anxious about what the future would now hold.

That experience further embedded what I'd learned for many years, which was not to talk about the "elephant in the middle of the room."

> ## That experience further embedded what I'd learned for many years, which was not to talk about the "elephant in the middle of the room."

I was 17 years old at the time, and years later, I'd realize the devastating impact my dad's departure *had*, and would *continue to have*, on me. I didn't see it at the time, but when he walked out of our home, he walked out on me, too.

I wondered if I'd somehow contributed to the problem; maybe I'd cost too much money, caused arguments, or done something else I shouldn't have. Or worse yet, maybe *I was the problem!* Without any resources to help me work through my thoughts and feelings, I was forced to stuff all of them inside.

Later that same year, I was preparing to graduate from high school and would be heading to the University of Iowa. Because my parents were separated, my dad was living in an apartment in a nearby town, though my mom and I lived in our family home about 15 minutes away.

With my high school graduation approaching, my dad asked me to meet him at the local Service Merchandise store in town. For a graduation gift, he helped me to pick out a stereo and speakers, which I was thrilled with. He helped me to load it into the family station wagon and then he got in his car and drove in the other direction back to his apartment. I drove home alone.

After arriving, I unloaded the stereo and speakers and carried them up to my bedroom. Once I took all the components out of their boxes, I realized I had *no idea* how to set it up. Nor did I have the confidence to attempt it on my own.

I knew I'd been given a generous gift, but at that moment, it felt worthless. I couldn't help but think that all the components not yet connected were a perfect representation of my family: individually we had our own strengths, but we remained disconnected.

Knowing my mom was also technically challenged; I just sat on the floor alone and cried. I'd never felt more alone. To this day I'm not sure how it happened, but a little later that afternoon our next-door neighbor, Ray Callahan, came over to our house. I don't know if my mom realized the predicament I was in and called him, or if he'd just stopped over for some other reason. Either way, he willingly came upstairs and got everything set up for me. Dr. Callahan, as I called him — he was an orthodontist *and* my best friend's dad — was a great man. He was kind and caring and always made me feel appreciated and included.

One day when his daughter Kenda and I were at their house, we baked some homemade sugar cookies. We ran into a problem though, because we got to talking and forgot to add the sugar to the dough! Certainly they'd tasted like paper towels! Nonetheless, Dr. Callahan ate several and raved about what good cooks we were. As usual, his reaction was so gracious and kind. Had the same thing happened in *my* home, I'd have likely heard they were a failure, and later they'd have been tossed in the garbage.

One summer afternoon during my senior year, I was out sunbathing in our backyard. My mom and three of her friends were in the middle of a tennis match. Just then my dad pulled up in our driveway and began carrying his belongings back into our house. I had no idea what was happening (nor did my mom), but we'd later learn that he'd decided to move back home. Again, just like his departure, there was no discussion about his return. *None!* We settled back into our normal everyday routines, and I began preparing to leave for college.

• • • • • • • • • • •

# SCENE 6: GO HAWKS OR GO HOME

That fall my parents packed me up and drove me to the University of Iowa's campus. As soon as they helped me unload the car and carry my belongings up to my dorm room, they got on their way back home. I shared a small room with two young girls who were complete strangers. One was a wild thing from a big city, and the other one was a very naïve girl from a small farming community. I was shell-shocked and had no idea of the coping skills that I hadn't developed and how that would make college extra difficult for me.

Also, I'd added more things to my ever-growing list of flaws. I believed that I wasn't smart enough, wasn't pretty enough, and didn't have what it took to fit in with others — although I wasn't even sure what that was. Nonetheless, I pledged a sorority, held a couple of leadership positions, and my junior year, made the University of Iowa cheerleading squad. Traveling with the team and cheering for the basketball and football games was a lot of fun. Maybe *too much* fun!

In addition to the fun, those were some difficult years. I felt lost in the shuffle and being one of 300 plus students in a class lecture allowed me to fade into the background. I had poor study habits — actually, I had no study habits.

Unfortunately, in my attempt to navigate those years I made a lot of mistakes; some were small mistakes that I learned from without too much collateral damage, while others were very traumatic. Unfortunately, I didn't have the type of relationship with either of my parents to be able to go to them and get the help I desperately needed. Instead, my experiences led to a drastic downward spiral. Numbing my pain with socializing, drinking, and doing *anything but studying* caused havoc on my class attendance, my grades, and my self-esteem.

Toward the end of my junior year, it all became too much, and I decided something had to change. The best solution I could come up with was to transfer to another college. Having made up my mind, I chose not to go out again for the cheerleading squad, resigned from the sorority leadership position, and prepared to move back home after the semester drew to a close.

My parents asked a few questions about my decision, but in the end they resigned themselves to the fact that I'd made up my mind. My best friend Kenda was in the same sorority and she, too, was ready for a change, so she decided to transfer with me. We both enrolled at Eastern Illinois University, and it felt like a chance for a fresh start.

At that time, had anyone asked me, I'd have said I was transferring to experience a smaller college setting. While it was true that I'd realized that the University of Iowa was way too big for me, there was more to the story — although I wouldn't have been able to put it into words at the time.

You see while I'd been in college, my parents' relationship continued to be tumultuous. I was naïve and full of hope that by being closer to home, I could do something to help them patch things up. (I didn't realize I was also *full* of lies — about who I was, what I was capable of, and who was responsible for my parents' relationship.)

I spent that summer living at home and working at my dad's office. In the fall I started classes at Eastern Illinois, which was just 40 minutes away. By transferring, I'd left behind the sorority house, the cheerleading squad, and some friends; however, my emotional clutter traveled with me — it now just lived on a different campus.

I did what I knew to do, which was to put on a happy face and get down to business. I moved into an old house on campus and lived with my childhood friend Tammy and four other girls I'd never met. Fortunately, the smaller college was a much better fit for me.

My dad had made it clear that he'd pay for four years of college but nothing more. So I did whatever it took to finish my Bachelor of Science degree; I buckled down and took 21 hours of credit *both* semesters of my senior year.

My activities at Eastern were drastically different than they'd been at the University of Iowa. I got serious about attending classes and studying, but didn't get involved with any extracurricular activities. I still found some time for socializing but with just a handful of friends, and I also worked at getting in shape and discovered the joy of running.

I graduated that May and moved to Des Moines, where I had accepted a job with an insurance company, Employers Mutual. I had no idea about my true interests and talents and therefore worked as a methods and procedures analyst. A little after a year, I added insult to injury and moved to a position as a computer programmer. I sat in a cubicle, writing computer coding. It was as if the oxygen was being sucked out of my lungs *every day*, and I hated it!

A year later I moved on and worked as an account representative in the publishing industry, and then as an office manager before starting my own sewing business several years later. Although I had a variety of jobs the common denominator was that they included a lot of people interaction and allowed me to use my creativity. I did a good job because I was a hard worker and always looked for additional ways I could contribute. Sadly though, I continued to feel anything but successful.

Eventually, I learned that the most damaging consequences of my past mistakes came from holding onto guilt and shame. (Coaching clients, I often share that guilt is feeling bad about something you've *done*. In contrast, shame is feeling bad about who you are. Shame goes much deeper and can have a more devastating impact.)

Many years later, as I decluttered my past, I no longer felt ashamed about myself as that young woman. In place of judgment and rejection, I learned to extend compassion, forgiveness, and grace to her — as I did to my parents. I came to see her as she really was, which was a lost and lonely little girl who was ill-equipped to handle so many aspects of young adulthood. As a result, I no longer carried the heavy baggage of shame.

Guilt and shame are heavy bags that we're not intended to carry.

---

**Guilt and shame are heavy bags that
we're not intended to carry.**

---

• • • • • • • • • • •

## SCENE 7: WEDDING DRESS SAGA

Not long after I graduated from college, my sister and her boyfriend Jack got engaged. Soon after, my mom, her good friend, my sister, and I all made a trip to Chicago; the trip was for one purpose: for my sister to find her wedding dress. She had appointments at Saks Fifth Avenue, Nordstrom, and Lord & Taylor.

We spent hours watching her try on dress after dress, and we'd "ooh and ah" over each one. We all gave our opinions to help her make her choice, and she settled on an elegant, form-fitting dress, with long, fitted sleeves of sheer lace. She looked beautiful in it, and the three-day shopping trip had been a success.

They were married in the fall of 1982, and by that time I'd been dating my boyfriend Ted for a couple of years. Ted was the most handsome man I'd ever met. More importantly, he was a man whom I could trust; he was kind, reliable, full of integrity, and he made me laugh. And he loved me. I couldn't have dreampt of anything more.

The following year, on a Saturday afternoon in August, Ted took me to see the national hot air balloon championship races. It was a beautiful sunny day, and we sat on the hood of his white 1975 Maverick. He popped a bottle of champagne and a question; he proposed, and I was thrilled. We'd been dating for nearly three years by then, and I'd been ready to take that step for quite a while.

After the proposal we drove over to his parents' house, and they shared in our exciting news. While there, I stepped into another room and called my dad to tell him the great news. I was so excited and told him that we were leaning toward getting married over the Thanksgiving weekend.

Nothing could have prepared me for his response; he said, "I hadn't planned on paying for another wedding so soon after your sister's." What? I felt like my heart dropped to my stomach! I was so disappointed and afraid that he'd potentially say we couldn't get married when we wanted to. Without having the tools to have a voice for myself, I did what I'd learned to do: I got to work and tried to make as few waves as possible.

Over the next few weeks we were busy planning our wedding. Because my parents had recently divorced and weren't exactly thrilled to have to talk with one another, I often felt caught in the middle of the communication. Also, because of my dad's initial comment about money, I tried to do everything I could on a budget — although I had no idea of the budget I had to work with.

As if that wasn't stressful enough, we ran into an issue as to where we'd get married. I'd grown up in the Episcopal Church in Champaign, Illinois, and ever since I was a little girl, I'd dreamed of walking down the long center aisle of our beautiful church.

Ted had been raised in the Greek Orthodox Church, in Des Moines, Iowa. When we met with his priest, we were told that unless we were married in a church that was Greek Orthodox, his church wouldn't acknowledge our marriage. In turn, that meant that when we'd eventually have kids, we wouldn't be able to baptize them in the Orthodox church, which was the church we planned on attending.

After considering having two weddings, one right after the other one, I gave in. To avoid making it a circus event, I agreed that we'd have just one wedding ceremony. It ended up being in my hometown, but in an Orthodox church that neither of us had ever been in before.

Rather than the beautiful wooden pews of my church, other than the few guests who had seats in the very small sanctuary of the Greek Church, nearly half of our guests were seated in folding chairs in the adjoining room — which was a basketball court! (Seriously! You can't make this stuff up!)

The wedding ceremony would be done partially in Greek, which meant I'd have no idea what was being said. Also, in a Greek Orthodox wedding, there are no wedding vows. The church's view is that the bride and groom have previously agreed to enter the covenant of marriage and, therefore, there's nothing more that needs to be said. (Years later, when I'd get upset about something, I'd joke with Ted that I never agreed to anything; I'd say, "I never said, 'I do!'")

Our reception would be held at the Champaign-Urbana Country Club, which certainly wasn't the cheapest place for a wedding reception; however, prestige was important, so my dad seemed completely fine with that expense.

As a way to save money, my mom suggested that I consider wearing my sister's wedding dress, and my sister graciously agreed to the idea. Looking back I wondered why someone didn't see the gross unfairness of the different approaches — the memorable three-day trip for my sister to select the wedding dress of her dreams, and my settling for wearing her hand-me-down dress.

In July of that year, Princess Diana married Prince Charles. Her unforgettable wedding dress had big puffy sleeves, and that gave my mom an idea. She talked with her seamstress about altering the sleeves of my sister's wedding dress, to look similar to Diana's. That way the dress would look a little different for me.

In the end, the seamstress took the narrow lace sleeves and replaced the top half with huge silk, puffy sleeves. In hindsight, this was not a good idea. It ended up being a dress I would never have chosen for myself in a million years. (Also, that meant my sister would no longer have her own wedding dress, which later made me very sad.)

My husband had his two brothers as best men, and half a dozen of his friends as ushers. One of my best friends, Tammy, was pregnant with her first child and was due the day of my wedding. Coupled with my concern about the wedding budget, I had my sister as my maid of honor and settled with two other friends being guest book attendants.

As of today, I've been happily married to Ted for 36 years, and I've thought about having a big party for our 40th anniversary. You might've already guessed, but I intend to go shopping for a very special dress — maybe even a wedding dress. I figure it's never too late to fulfill a few of my unmet dreams.

* * * * * * * * * * * *

## SCENE 8: MY BIG FAT GREEK FAMILY

When I married Ted, I knew that I was crazy in love with him, and I believed we'd have a wonderful life together. Yet I had no idea of the impact his family would have on me. Ted's parents were both of Greek heritage, and his dad John had spent the majority of his upbringing in Greece. I knew nothing about the Greek culture; I hadn't eaten Baklava or Pastitsio or any other Greek dishes, but I quickly fell in love with my new family and most of the food. (If you've seen the movie "My Big Fat Greek Wedding," that's a pretty accurate portrayal of our Greek family.)

My mother-in-law, Rose, made me feel like I was the daughter she'd never had, and she admitted that although she certainly loved all three of their sons, she'd always hoped for a girl. She was my greatest cheerleader, and later, after we had kids, she championed anything that any one of her six grandchildren were involved with. In her role as a Yia Yia ("grandmother" in Greek) she was the best! Sometimes I knew she loved them so much (and us too) that I thought her heart might burst.

Years later I would often share that Rose set the bar for being the best mother-in-law, and I hoped that someday I could be half as good to my future daughter-in-law. She was a tough act to follow!

John, my father-in-law, also gave me a warm welcome. I'd been so wounded and shamed for my enthusiasm and energy, yet he applauded me for it. He believed in me and encouraged me. With his unwavering love and support, he unknowingly helped me to understand the concept of God's unconditional love for us as His children. Through my relationship with both of my in-laws, God provided salve for many of my emotional wounds.

In many ways our families couldn't have been any more different. While I'd grown up with just one sister, Ted had two brothers. In my family, conversations were often awkward and physical affection was rare, whereas Ted's family talked comfortably and freely demonstrated their love and affection for one another.

In addition, after going to medical and dental school, my dad had become a doctor; Ted's dad John graduated from high school and owned and operated five Coney Island restaurants.

My mother was known for being impeccably dressed (even if only going to the mailbox) and was extremely proper in everything she did. In contrast, Ted's mom Rose dressed in more casual clothes and comfortable shoes and was as warm and down to earth as anyone you could ever meet.

Another big difference was in our families' approach to mealtimes. For dinner we'd often have spaghetti or chicken, and nothing but salt and pepper were used for seasoning. Also, if you wanted something at the dinner table you would politely ask for it to please be passed to you.

Ted's family often had Greek foods like lamb and fish, and they'd use a lot of garlic, oregano, and other seasonings. Also, on occasion (even though it'd make Rose cringe), when Ted would ask for something like a roll, one of his brothers would literally toss it to him! Mealtimes were fun and always included lively conversation and delicious food. For the next few decades, almost every Sunday evening, we'd go to their house to eat dinner, and those are some of my favorite memories with them.

• • • • • • • • • • •

# SCENE 9: WANTING A BABY

In 1986, Ted and I'd been married for two and a half years. We were ready to start our family but weren't having any success. My sister and many of my girlfriends were getting pregnant as soon as they wanted to, but not me. Worse yet, no one was talking about the topic of infertility.

For a solid year it felt like I was on an emotional roller coaster. I'd get my hopes up only to have them dashed the following month. I was so frustrated and disappointed, and I felt defective — even though they'd run multiple tests on both Ted and me and found nothing to explain our infertility. Up to that point in my life, that was one of the hardest things I'd faced.

I'd always had a dream of having two children, two years apart. God had a different plan. After going through countless infertility treatments and eventually a surgery, we had two wonderful children four and a half years apart. God's plan was much better than my own, but I didn't have a way of knowing that at the time.

Our daughter Kristin was born with a birth defect called Microtia; it's a birth deformity that's extremely rare but affected her right ear. At her birth, it looked as if her right ear was folded over. However, in addition to having a malformed outer ear, her inner ear bones were fused together. That meant she'd have a significant hearing loss in that one ear.

We went first to the University of Iowa Hospital. We were told that with two or three surgeries the doctors should be able to create an inner ear canal and the framework for an outer ear and restore her hearing. Going into the first two surgeries our hopes were high, but things didn't go as planned. Problems kept developing with healing, and Kristin ended up having 19 surgical procedures! Most were in Iowa City, but she even had two surgeries in Children's Hospital in Los Angeles, CA.

Many of her surgeries required staying in the hospital (sometimes for a week or more) and were extremely challenging for a young girl. Ultimately, when she was a junior in high school, we found a solution.

We learned about Robert Barron on an episode of the Oprah show in which he was featured. "Bob" had previously worked for the CIA making disguises for prominent government officials, and had moved into making prosthetics for children and adults who had issues similar to Kristin's.

After two more trips and another surgery in Bethesda, MD, Bob created a prosthetic ear for Kristin. Wearing it improved her hearing considerably. It also allowed her to wear sunglasses and two earrings, which understandably, was a big deal to her. (Like most people, you've probably never thought about the benefits of having two ears, as opposed to just one.)

Those years were hard on all of us, Kristin, our son John, Ted, and me; however, one tremendous thing came in the middle of those struggles. When Kristin was 12 years old and was struggling with all that was happening, God began to get a hold of her heart — and soon after, mine, too.

And that's a perfect segue to the next act.

# ACT 2

## *My Relationship with God*

In the First Act of my story I shared about my *emotional* development. Now it's time for the Second Act, which is about my *spiritual* development. Although I'd initially believed *in* God, I learned to *believe God*. I'd never have guessed the difference between the two, nor the impact it would have on my life. As God guided me through many of life's toughest challenges, I grew to have a personal, vibrant relationship with Him, and I'll show you how you can, too.

• • • • • • • • • • •

## SCENE 1: A MEANINGLESS CHORE

I grew up in the sixties and seventies being forced to go to church. Nearly every Sunday I'd put up resistance to attending the Episcopal Church. I dreaded having to go for a variety of reasons; I hated having to get dressed up in nice clothes, I hated having to sit quietly in uncomfortable wooden pews; and I didn't go to school with the kids that attended Sunday school, so I never felt like I fit in.

I remember one time my dad was so fed up with my attitude about church, I was "punished." He gave me the assignment of writing a three-page essay about the importance of going to church. I dutifully wrote what I knew was expected, and yet concluded my essay with one final sentence: "You still can't make me *like* church!" (Obviously, this was evidence of my independent streak showing up, even as a youngster.)

Looking back, I realized that to my family, church was nothing more than another chore; going to church was something you were *supposed* to do — much like making your bed, brushing your teeth, or taking the garbage to the curb. It was something to be marked off the list before moving on to something else.

Even as a young adult, I begrudgingly went when I was home from college for the holidays, but otherwise, I never gave church a thought. My apathy toward church remained until 1983.

My boyfriend at the time who became my husband, Ted Economos, had been raised in the Greek Orthodox Church in Des Moines. The church services were similar to those in the Episcopal church in my hometown: traditional and symbolic, and, I thought, rather "dry;" however, because his church was very important to him and I'd moved to Des Moines, attending the Greek church seemed like the right thing to do.

Thanksgiving weekend of that year, we were married in a Greek Orthodox church. Then, four years later, in 1987 we had a baby girl, Kristin. Another four and a half years later, in 1991, we had a baby boy, John. We had both of our children baptized in the church, as was expected.

As a family, we attended the Greek Orthodox church for over a decade; but since at least half of the service was done in Greek, our kids and I didn't understand it. Consequently, we got *nothing* meaningful out of attending.

• • • • • • • • • • • •

## SCENE 2: A NEW BELIEVER

In the summer of 1999, I was about to turn 40 years old and our daughter Kristin had recently turned 12. One evening she and I ended up attending a speaking event at a local church, New Hope Assembly of God. While we were listening to a young intern share her message, something significant happened to me — *and* to Kristin!

When the two of us got back in the car to drive home, she said she wanted to go to a church like that one; she said she'd felt something different and that it felt really good. As she continued sharing her feelings with me, tears began streaming down *my* face. I, too, felt something I could hardly put into words. Later, I realized what we'd felt was the Holy Spirit; and we'd never experienced anything like it before.

From that point on, the two of us regularly attended New Hope, where our faith took root and began to grow. Kristin and I benefited greatly from Pastor Weaver's powerful sermons, the lively and gifted choir and their incredible music productions, and the warmth of the congregation. I was often brought to tears, as a result of experiencing the love and joy of people vibrantly alive and deeply connected to God.

Meanwhile, Ted and John continued to attend the Greek Orthodox Church, which was hard on all of us. None of us liked heading in different directions on Sunday mornings, but we continued for the time being.

I periodically invited Ted to join us, but I knew it was vastly different than the symbolic, traditional service he'd grown accustomed to. Eventually, Ted and John would occasionally join us, but *it never failed* — it would inevitably be a day when a guest speaker would give a *dramatic* testimony that made all four of us uncomfortable.

Kristin and I attended Sunday school and began learning what it meant to have a relationship with Christ. I participated in my first Bible study and purchased a Bible, even though it felt strange and scripture was all so new to me. (I also bought a children's Bible so I could familiarize myself with the most basic of stories, since I'd not grown up with them.)

For a period of time, I'd felt bad about how much I'd missed out on since I'd not been taught about a relationship with Christ. Eventually, however, I became grateful that I didn't have a lot of "religiosity" to have to dig out from under.

The church had a music library where you could check out CDs, and I took full advantage of the opportunity. I would blast tunes in my car (by CeCe Winans, Deniece Williams, and others) and sing along, often crying from the connection I felt with God through the songs.

Later, "My Father's Eyes" by Amy Grant, "Jesus Take the Wheel" by Carrie Underwood, and "Shackles," by Mary Mary became some of my all-time favorites, and they fueled my passion for Christ.

God also provided friends with a strong faith, like Kelly, whose biblical knowledge and relationship with God was a source of inspiration for me. I can't count the number of times she'd give me a CD or a book that seemed to be sent by God himself, as it was exactly what I needed to help grow my faith. (Never underestimate the impact providing something like that can have on a person's faith. It really can be very powerful.)

While still having a fairly new faith I had an experience I'll never forget. John was seven years old, and he'd been very scared about losing what was already a *very* loose tooth. He and I were sitting in our parked car that afternoon, waiting for Ted to come out of the grocery store. John unlatched his seatbelt and crawled over the console and into my lap.

Although I'd not previously had the confidence to pray for what I considered small things, I wrapped John in my arms and did so. I shared with God that He knew how scared John was about pulling his tooth. Also, I acknowledged and gave thanks for God's presence right there with us, and I asked Him to provide whatever He knew John needed.

When I finished my prayer, John began to tell me something and while doing so, reached up and touched his loose tooth. At that very moment, it literally dropped into his hand! His eyes were as big as saucers! So were mine. That was an unforgettable day, not because his tooth fell out, but because in that instant his faith began to grow, as did mine.

I was learning that it's okay to share our wants and needs with God, and that nothing is too small to bring to Him. Although He's not a genie in a bottle who grants all our wishes, He loves to give us the desires of our heart. Even better, is that as we draw closer to Him, *His* heart's desires become our heart's desires.

---

**Delight yourself in the Lord and He will give you
the desires of your heart. For God is working in you,
giving you the desires of His heart.
(Psalm 37:4 and Philippians 2:13)**

---

As a new believer, my faith and my beliefs were soon put to the test. Shortly after the experience with John's loose tooth, I'd gone to see a dermatologist to have a couple of moles checked out. After the doctor assured me that none of them met the criteria to be problematic, I hesitated, and *something* made me go ahead and ask that one in particular be removed.

Several days later the doctor's office called me and shared the news; I had Clark's level four melanoma! At that time, melanoma (skin cancer) was considered the deadliest kind of cancer. Although the diagnosis was scary, I had an unusual sense of peace. (I'd later realize that was my newly formed faith, trusting God would take care of what I needed — which He did.)

(To be clear, Clark's level is a staging system, from one to five, based on how many layers of skin the cancer has penetrated. It is quite different than *stage four*, which would mean the cancer had spread throughout the body and would be even more alarming.)

Two days later I had surgery, and they removed a good-sized chunk of my right calf to ensure they got clean margins. I was sent home from the hospital with strict instructions that I was to rest, with my leg elevated *above my heart*. That meant that I'd need to be in a horizontal position on the couch.

At that time I owned and operated a sewing business out of our home. I sewed window treatments, bedding, pillows, and other interior design products for my clients and other designers. Also at that time, I still believed a lot of lies: I believed that my value was based on the amount of work I got done, I believed others' needs were more important than my own, and I didn't yet understand the concept of healthy boundaries and self-care. Consequently, I justified some sad and ridiculous behavior.

I'd given my word to a client that I'd have her cushions finished (for the patio of her *second home*), within the next few days — although I hadn't counted on having a cancer diagnosis and surgery during that time. But that didn't matter to me. I felt I *had* to keep my word and get the cushions finished as I'd agreed to.

So I got everything situated on the couch, having my leg propped up on half a dozen pillows. I then twisted my upper body to hang over the side of the couch to finish hand sewing her cushions. (I know. That's *crazy!* But given my mindset about my value and work, it made perfect sense. Our mindsets allow us to justify some pretty crazy things.)

Fortunately, through the decluttering process, I learned that my value has nothing to do with what I accomplish and that my needs are just as important as others'. And eventually, that allowed me to maintain healthy boundaries for myself, which allowed me to make self-care a priority.

• • • • • • • • • • •

# SCENE 3: HEARING GOD AT A COMEDY SHOW

I've literally *heard* God's voice only one time, but it was certainly unforgettable. In the fall of 2000, along with my sister and my friend Lynn, I attended a concert of Christian comedian Chonda Pierce. That night, as a fairly new believer in Christ, I found myself impacted by what she shared; she told stories, some tragic and others hilarious, about her family, herself and God. In the process, she moved the audience to laughter, tears, *and action,* for Jesus. That's when I clearly heard a male voice say, "You're going to do that."

I nearly jumped out of my skin! Turning to see who'd spoken, and seeing no one, I looked to see if my friends had any reaction. Oblivious to my "God moment" they were engrossed in what Chonda was sharing. It appeared that I was the only one who heard God speak, and His words were for *me.*

Certainly He must have been mistaken. For 40 years I'd believed so much junk about myself that I figured I'd be the *last* person to stand in front of an audience and speak about *anything.* But God doesn't make mistakes.

It would be *years* after attending Chonda's concert before I came to understand God's original statement; I was to share my own stories and insights with others. Over time, I learned that my inabilities and insecurities weren't even a factor. It was about God and *His strength and His plans.*

• • • • • • • • • • •

# SCENE 4: A BAD AND GOOD HOMECOMING

Unfortunately, for those of us who become parents, we inevitably pass on to our own children at least *some* of the emotional baggage from our parents. In addition, we manage to accumulate some clutter from our own experiences, which only adds to that baggage.

In 2005, when Kristin was a senior in high school, she came home with the news that she'd been voted to be on the homecoming court. Unfortunately, I had some unfinished business about *my own* homecoming experience that'd been hanging around for decades.

You see when I was a senior in high school; my good friends were nominated for the homecoming court. I was not. Even though I'd not really thought I had *any* chance, I was still disappointed and felt left out. I came home from school that day, and although my mom knew it was the day of voting for the court, nothing was said. Sadly, those stuffed feelings of disappointment had hardened. When Kristin came home and shared that she'd been selected for the homecoming court I said, "Well, that's good," but I did so with a tone that was anything but convincing.

While she was eating a quick snack before heading out the door to an activity, we continued to talk. She shared her disappointment that one of her good friends hadn't been voted onto the court, and that prompted me to say that I thought they should consider eliminating the homecoming court tradition, because it was nothing more than a popularity contest — and that *many* other girls would be left out and feel bad. (I know what I said was horrible, but it was directly tied to the crusty scab that was covering my emotional wound. Thankfully, it was soon to come off.)

After she left the house I went on a walk with a neighborhood friend, and she helped me to see my "unfinished business" about homecoming. In addition, after I crawled into bed that night and prayed, God convicted me of the error in my thinking and He allowed me to think about myself as the young high-school girl that I'd been. As I sorted out my own experience, I saw things more clearly and so the next morning I sat down at breakfast and talked about it with Kristin.

I told her that I'd realized my reaction was about myself at that age, and that not only did I think it was great that she was nominated, but that I thought there'd be no one better to represent her high school. I meant *every word* of what I said from the bottom of my heart, and I could see by the expression on her face that my words had made a big difference. She left for school, and I felt a great sense of relief; for maybe the very first time I felt like I'd been able to retrieve the arrow I'd unintentionally flung at her heart *before* it did significant damage.

Due to Kristin's schedule (school, student council, her job, church, dance classes, and singing lessons), she'd have no time that week to go shopping for homecoming dresses. Consequently, that chore would be left up to me.

The next night I prayed and asked God to provide two dresses; she'd need one for the daytime coronation ceremony at the high school, and a more formal one for the actual homecoming dance. I reminded God that we were on a budget (like He didn't know), so they needed to be affordable.

Much like many other mother-daughter relationships, Kristin and I didn't always see eye to eye. So, I knew it'd take a miracle for me to pick out even *one* dress that she'd like, let alone *two!* But I figured I'd give it my best shot.

The next day I went to the local department store, Younkers, and started searching. Fairly quickly I found a cute, short, black dress with turquoise piping around the neck and bustline. It was the right size, *and* it was on the sale rack.

After looking for quite a while longer (for a long dress for the dance), I was about ready to give up but at the last minute something caught my eye. It was a burgundy, floor-length gown with beautiful beading on the front of the halter dress — and this one was on the clearance rack! I practically *skipped* out of the store, excited to have Kristin see them.

When she flew in the door in between her school activities and dance classes, she tried them both on. It *was* a miracle; they looked beautiful on her, fit like they were custom made, and she loved both of them!

Three days later, she was voted homecoming queen. The jeweled crown looked great with both of the dresses and best of all, with God's help, that particular wound of mine would no longer cause damage to either one of us.

This was a classic example of how the wounds we carry can unintentionally hurt others, who are often the people we love the most. Hence, the importance of decluttering our past so it doesn't continue to cause damage to *anyone*, including ourselves.

As I shared previously, we're wise to forgive our parents for the damage they unintentionally caused us, and we must do the same for ourselves.

We must forgive ourselves and accept God's grace for the damage we've done in parenting our own children. It works both ways.

I've been very fortunate to have received healing that God provided on my wounds from previous generations. I've also witnessed first-hand, God providing salve to the wounds of my own children. God's Word says it this way: God will restore the years the locusts ate. (Joel 2:25) You can rest assured that God never wastes even the tiniest morsel of what we've gone through, and He can, *and usually does*, bring something good out of it.

---

**"And we know that God causes all things to work together for good to those who know God and are called according to His purpose."**
**(Romans 8:28)**

---

Over the next decade, we attended a new church, Valley Evangelical Free, and my faith continued to grow. During that time, I stepped up my game. I was no longer limiting my involvement to just attending church. I got involved with several Beth Moore Bible studies and devoured books by Joyce Meyers, Max Lucado, and others. Also, I branched out and went through a program called Christ Life Solution, eventually becoming one of its facilitators. One thing leads to another. Soon I was working at the headquarters of this organization.

I ended up being involved with Christ Life's ministry for ten years. Throughout that time I benefited greatly from sound Biblical teachings, mentoring, and coaching. At times I felt like an adult with a kindergartener's faith among others who had a master's degree in it, but over time, God began to give me an insatiable appetite for His Word and His presence.

---

**God began to give me an insatiable appetite for His Word and His presence.**

---

While teaching some of the Christ Life classes at a local church, Lutheran Church of Hope, I found myself drawn to worship there. It was a huge church, but I'd never heard a more dynamic and captivating pastor (Mike Householder) and the sermons stuck with me, which was highly unusual.

It wasn't long before our entire family felt right at home in the midst of several thousand worshipers. People literally stood in line to get into the church services on Sunday mornings, even though eventually there were five services from which to choose. It was evident that the Holy Spirit was alive and well at Hope, and our faith grew by leaps and bounds.

• • • • • • • • • • •

# SCENE 5: GIVING BIRTH TO WHOLEHEARTED LIVING

By 2010, my faith had grown tremendously. I no longer believed that God was too busy to talk with me or that He was disappointed in me and, consequently, I found it much easier to connect with Him. I also learned to ask for what I needed and wanted, but ultimately for *His will*, rather than mine.

Somewhere along the line I began praying before going to sleep, asking God to speak to me through my dreams. (Since I'm a "talker," I kid around and say that I think God speaks to me the most when I'm sleeping, because that's when He's more likely to get a word in!)

Not always, but often, I'd wake up with a vivid dream, which was a direct answer to my prayers. One morning I woke up with a dream that felt crucial to remember, so I described it in my journal.

In that dream, I was returning from somewhere in my car, and I'd pulled up in front of our house. I was shocked to see several huge bulldozers in our front yard, and they were digging up most of the dirt and transferring it into a truck bed (to be hauled away later). Upon waking, I asked God to show me what the dream meant. Over the next few days it became apparent to me: God was doing some excavation work in my life and was preparing me for some big changes.

A few days later, I had another vivid dream that I also jotted down. In that one, much shorter than the first, I was in labor and giving birth. However, it didn't seem to be a child that I was birthing. (That was reassuring because we already had two and, though they were great, that was all I thought I could manage.)

At the same time (when I wasn't sleeping) I began to feel a stirring deep inside. Over the series of a few months, God provided a vision. He showed me how much women could accomplish if they learned to get out of their own way and claim their true identities (who they were created to be in Christ). He showed me how they could change their families, their communities, and ultimately the world. (No kidding! I quickly learned that God's dreams are *way* bigger than anything I'd ever come up with.)

Meanwhile, Ted had been looking for a job change for over six months. Even though my job was part-time, it provided regular income that made a difference to our household budget. Despite that fact, Ted and I agreed that I should say "yes" to what God was prompting me to do.

The next day, I resigned from my job at Christ Life and dove into what I felt God was putting on my heart, which was to start a business called Wholehearted Living. At that time, I envisioned being a coach of some kind, helping women to get emotionally and physically fit. I pictured walking with clients to help them build up their endurance while also coaching them to work through their past and present frustrations or concerns. Fortunately, as God so often does, He revealed just a small portion of what He would later lead me to do. At that time had I seen the enormity of it, I might have run for cover!

I was excited, but also apprehensive. I didn't think I was qualified, but I soon learned that God doesn't call the qualified, but He qualifies those He calls. And make no mistake about it; He calls each one of us.

---

 **. . . God doesn't call the qualified, but He qualifies those He calls. And make no mistake about it; He calls each one of us.**

---

Putting aside my fears and limiting beliefs (about who I was and what I was capable of), I began typing. For several weeks I did practically nothing other than type the download I was receiving from God. I had no idea what might become of this, but I was convinced I had to get it out of my head and onto paper. As I did, God began to show me the impact these materials could have on women; how they could help women to declutter their lives emotionally, physically *and spiritually.*

During that time, I got together with Tracy, who was an incredible woman whom I'd just recently met. We gathered at Panera Bread to get better acquainted, and as we did, I shared the vision God had shown me. She shared that she also felt a deep conviction that this was the start of something *big*, and that she was committed to help in any way she could. Little did we know how big it really was. At that point I described the vision from God as deliciously frightening!

Before long, several women reached out with interest in what I'd been working on. As I shared about the writing exercises I was drafting they agreed to be my first clients. Some weeks, *literally* as they were arriving at our house, the day's lesson was still being printed. (Talk about "fresh off the press!")

The four of us sat around our kitchen table for several months, and in the process of going through the materials we experienced significant growth. One woman was able to drop the guilt of her divorce, while another shed the heavy weight of shame from previous sexual activity. Still another left behind the toxic beliefs that she wasn't "good enough," and learned to value who she really was. Similarly, I found myself dropping the deep shame I'd carried for way too long, and rather than disliking who I was, learned to celebrate the woman God had created in *me*. To say it was life changing for all of us would be an understatement.

Over the next several years God continued to guide me and to provide exactly what was needed to develop the Wholehearted Living program. So often at the very moment that I realized a need for the next step, the provision would appear right in front of me. However, that didn't mean it was effortless or easy to continue doing what I felt God had asked me to do.

For example, while my endless energy and drive helped me to persevere (to fulfill the vision God had provided to me in 2010), it also was challeng-ing for a few of my team members; my need for change was frustrating for some and consequently they moved on to other things. And sometimes that was hard on me.

In addition, although my excitement about the program never waned, I saw that it dropped off significantly for several others who were coaching for the program. As my mentor put it, "It's your baby and no one else is going to love it like you do." Coming to grips with that was hard — especially since the thought of doing it alone felt overwhelming to me.

Along the way I learned a lot, including how to give myself grace to learn from my mistakes, rather than emotionally beating myself up about them; I learned how to celebrate my enthusiasm, creativity, and energy and at the same time to learn where and when it needed to be managed carefully.

Somewhere along the lines God led me to my life's purpose, which is to "enthusiastically encourage others to live *wholeheartedly*, by discovering their true identities and pursuing their purposes with passion." He also led me to publish the material I'd been using with coaching clients as a series of three books that became the curriculum for the Wholehearted Living program: *Your Relationship with Yourself, Your Relationship with Cravings, and Your Relationship with God.*

After doing so, through a series of God-orchestrated introductions, I got connected with a wonderful Christian man, Dr. Paul Leavenworth. He had a seminary degree, years of experience teaching and mentoring, and came into my life at just the right time. Initially, I hired him to take me through a workbook that he had written called, *The Extraordinary Power of a Focused Life.*

After completing that first workbook, accompanied by Paul's weekly coaching, I participated in several of his workshops and subsequently enrolled in a distance learning program through New Hope College. I completed a series of undergraduate courses, all taught by Paul, and my studies culminated in earning a CLC (Christian Leadership Certificate). Paul's knowledge and methods of delivery were a perfect match, and they made learning about the Christian faith exciting and rewarding. Despite the fact that I'd hated studying in school, thanks in large part to Paul, I discovered a love for studying God's Words. Consequently, my faith grew by leaps and bounds.

For the next *six years*, I poured my time, energy, and money into further developing the Wholehearted Living program. For example, I created a variety of workshops that allowed women to get a taste of the program before choosing to invest in themselves with the time and money that the program required. Even though I knew how quickly any one of them would make the same investment for one of their own kids, I understood that many women needed to dip their toes in the water before jumping in. In addition, as we gained more clients we needed more help, so I continued to add members to our team. Eventually, I supported a team of 12 women; all of them had completed the WL courses and had experienced significant changes in their own lives and wanted to help others to experience the same. The majority of our team members worked as heart coaches and were responsible for arranging and facilitating the weekly small-group coaching sessions.

In addition, several others volunteered their time to help me advance the business. We added a prayer committee, a director of alums, a technical administrator, a bookkeeper and a board of directors.

I also began expanding the program to other locations, like Owatonna, MN, and Red Oak and Cedar Rapids, both in Iowa. It was *a lot* of hard work, but throughout it all I experienced God's amazing provision. His timing and His plans often blew me away, and as a result, my relationship with Him was greater than I could've ever imagined.

• • • • • • • • • • •

## SCENE 6: BLIND-SIDED

In the summer of 2016, Ted had complained of feeling a little tired, and at his annual physical he learned that his blood sugar was high. Although he certainly wasn't overweight, nor did it run in his family, his general practitioner strongly suggested getting him on pre-diabetic medicine.

Ted had recently had a knee replacement, and so he thought the lack of exercise might have had something to do with it. Three months later, after exercising and cleaning up his diet, his blood sugar had dropped, but not enough to satisfy the doctor, so he was put on a medication. I'd expressed my concern about treating the blood sugar before doing more tests to get to the bottom of why it had risen, but the doctor's prescribed treatment weighed heavily on Ted, and so he decided to take the medicine.

Over the next few months Ted didn't feel great; it wasn't that he felt bad, but he didn't feel like his usual self and sometimes shared that he'd had a queasy stomach. After talking it over with his doctor the dosage was changed, but no more tests were run. Ted continued to be involved with his usual activities: He worked full-time, exercised three to four times a week, cooked most of our meals, served on a couple of boards, went to church, and kept up with mowing the lawn and other house projects. But we were about to be blind-sided.

On the afternoon of April 4, 2017, Ted and I were sitting in the exam room of an internal medicine doctor we'd been referred to. The past few days he'd undergone a series of tests, and we were there to get the results. When the doctor sat down in his chair and then scooted himself a bit closer to us, I could feel a sick feeling of dread rising in the pit of my stomach. Little did we know that our world was about to be turned upside down.

The prior week we'd been on a fabulous vacation in beautiful Grand Cayman. Despite the serene environment, rather than feeling rested and refreshed, Ted had complained of feeling really tired and having an occasional sour stomach. We commented to each other that at 58 years old, who *doesn't* feel fatigued and have an occasional upset stomach. Therefore, *nothing* could have prepared us for the words that came out of the doctor's mouth:

---

### "Ted, I'm sorry to have to tell you, but you have stage four pancreatic cancer."

---

I felt like the wind had been sucked out of my lungs. I couldn't breathe. Ted had all the components of a healthy life: he'd exercised regularly, eaten a healthy Mediterranean diet, and had a deep faith, a close-knit family, and great friends. Sad to say, all of his "clean living" did nothing to change the bad news. The doctor went on to explain that the cancer had started in the pancreas and had already spread to both lobes of his liver. In fact, these intrusive tumors now took up residence in his liver, occupying 45 percent of it!

Though stunned to the core, we somehow managed to ask some questions. Finally, in an attempt to find *something* to hold onto, I asked,"

What kind of a timeline are you talking about?" The doctor looked down, sighed, and replied somberly, "Maybe months to a year."

These words reeled me into what felt like an out-of-body experience. I just knew this had to be a mistake! I felt numb as I tried to absorb the horrific blow. Consequently, I didn't remember much else that was said.

Once out of the doctor's office, Ted and I got to the car where we fell into a hugging, sobbing mess. I couldn't believe or accept this news. The fear of losing him seemed too much to even *think* about!

After some time, we decided to head home. Since we'd taken two cars, I got into mine and began following him home, which was a strange blessing in itself. I'm a verbal processor, so on my drive I called one of my best friends, Kelly, and told her the devastating news. She'd been praying for our visit, and she's one of the most comforting people. Kelly has the rare talent of listening with her whole heart without trying to fix anything or give advice. She makes it safe to process *anything* I'm going through.

When I shared Ted's diagnosis with her and mentioned the doctor's projected timeframe, she sobbed right along with me. I told her it looked like I might be a widow before I was even 58 years old, and the *thought* of that was terrifying to me!

As word traveled about Ted's horrific diagnosis, friends began to reach out. In an attempt to streamline a way to communicate the latest updates, Ted agreed to my establishing a blog to share. At his suggestion, it was titled "Faith vs. Fear." Little did we know then how appropriate that title would become for *all* of us.

• • • • • • • • • • • •

## SCENE 7: TRUSTING GOD WITH CANCER

A few days after hearing of Ted's diagnosis, I was still trying to digest the news. I kept thinking about our future and how different that might end up looking, given his pancreatic cancer. Some people might think about the future with their spouse and focus on traveling or owning a second home.

However, so often when we'd see little kids, Ted would comment on how cute they were and how much fun it would be *someday*, to be a "Pa Pou" (which is the Greek word for "grandfather"). So I found myself pleading with God, asking Him not to deny Ted that privilege since it was truly a dream of his.

Little did I know the significance of my concern about Ted not becoming a grandfather. The issue would resurface, but not in the way you might think.

Fortunately, over the next day or two, God reminded me that He was capable of miraculous things. As a result, despite it already being stage four, I came back to the belief that He could heal Ted (but I wasn't sure that He *would*).

The following week God helped me to make a transition; He led me to the various scriptures that pertain to healing, and I dug into each one. I also began praying about them and talking about them with my trusted confidants, Kelly and Denise, two of my best friends who know a lot about scripture *and* a lot about me. The accumulation of all of that provided overwhelming evidence that Jesus healed many people and that He was still in the miracle business.

Through that transition, which I have no doubt God orchestrated, things felt much less heavy. I felt hopeful and began to trust that God would, in fact, heal Ted — although I doubted that it'd be a short or easy journey.

---

**Bartimaeus threw aside his coat, jumped up, came to Jesus. "What do you want me to do for you?" Jesus asked. "My Rabbi, the blind man said, "I want to see!" And Jesus said to him, "Go, for your faith has healed you." Instantly the man could see, and he followed Jesus down the road. (Mark 10:50-52)**

---

I'm a visual person, and one day I began to think of God being the manager in a business that I worked in. Whenever I'd have a concern, I'd send him an email and ask that He let me know if and when He wanted me to do anything more on that particular subject.

However, I often found myself in my imagination walking back down the hall and poking my head into His office to add some small detail that wasn't important. My impatience and lack of faith caused me to keep checking on the status of the matter. It was a process, but eventually I got much better at leaving things in His hands and keeping my hands off!

Over the past decade, when I'd find myself struggling I'd ask for encouragement or confirmation of God's presence and direction for my life. In response, He'd often provide a deer in my path. In fact, the day I resigned from my previous job and started to develop Wholehearted Living, I prayed; I asked that God's plan and provision would be evident as I took this leap of faith.

No sooner than I'd finished my prayer, I looked out our front window. (We live in an active neighborhood in a suburb of Des Moines). There, right at the end of our driveway, was one adult deer. She was staring in my direction, and I literally gasped out loud. It was another of what I called a "God wink;" it was evidence that He'd heard me, and He was right there with me.

I was anxious about Ted's doctor's appointment later that morning, so I decided to go for a run beforehand. It was drizzling rain and on my run I cried out to God and told Him that I didn't want Ted to have to have traditional chemotherapy that would more than likely be part of his treatment protocol; however, I also prayed that God would provide exactly what was necessary for healing Ted's body.

As I released my will for God's, I rounded the corner of the bike path on which I'd been running. There, not eight feet from me, was . . . you guessed it, a beautiful deer! The deer was lying down but looked directly at me as I ran by. I was overcome with God's love and His perfect way to show me, once again, that He was right there *with me* and *for me*. I sobbed the rest of my run but came home with a peace that God had the perfect provision for us.

Within the first few minutes of meeting Ted's oncologist, Dr. Buroker, we felt much better about Ted's cancer. Eventually, we'd come to realize that he was, without a doubt, a gift straight from Heaven!

Dr. Buroker, "Tom" as he told us to call him, asked us what we'd already heard about Ted's condition, and I quickly told him that we'd been told he likely only had months to a year to live. He immediately frowned, shook his head, and said, "Hell! We haven't even been up to bat yet!" His words were the most comforting of any we could've imagined.

He told us that although there wasn't a cure for neuroendocrine pancreatic cancer (not yet anyway), there were a variety of treatments. In his words, "We'll choose a horse and ride it as long as it's doing what we need it to do. When it stops working, we'll choose a different horse."

Dr. Buroker was a confident, kind, compassionate, patient, and humble man. At our request, he sent Ted's medical records to the Mayo Clinic in Rochester, MN, to have their oncology team review them. Then, based upon their recommendations, together we'd establish a treatment plan.

We looked forward to our visits with Tom. His well-timed one-liners, some occasional colorful language, and always parting with a heartfelt, "God bless you" — all were perfectly timed. Tom never failed to provide the knowledge, the outlook, and the hope that we needed most, and it truly was the best medicine of all.

• • • • • • • • • • • •

## SCENE 8: RAIN, RAIN, GO AWAY!

Just five days later, we experienced the reality of the expression, "When it rains it pours." Several nights earlier, there'd been a huge rainstorm with a lot of wind. The following few days, I'd walked by our bedroom closet and found the carpet a bit damp. Upon further investigation, it became obvious that we'd had a leak somewhere and that water had actually been running down the wall of our bedroom.

I called to have our handyman come to investigate the source of the damage. Within a short time he discovered there was a seam in the exterior siding that wasn't adequately sealed. Therefore, with the intense rain and wind, the water had an easy entrance.

Unfortunately, the water had also run down the wall in the dining room on our main floor. In addition, the flooring was damaged and would therefore need to be replaced. The extent of the damage was overwhelming, especially given our current focus on Ted's very recent diagnosis.

The next several days, I began making numerous calls to our homeowners insurance company, a restoration company, carpet company, drywaller, and more. The next day, after the sections of the damaged drywall were removed, we discovered ants . . . a lot of *big, dark, ants!*

My next call was to an exterminator. He determined the ants had probably come from a tree right outside the biggest window in our bedroom (a few feet away from the damaged siding). That meant we had to call and have our tree removed. They ended up having to also grind the entire stump, which left us with a *mountain* of mulch that had to be removed.

Our good friend, Larry, was my next call. Within hours he pulled up in a pickup truck and began shoveling the mulch into his truck bed. It took two separate trips, but Larry removed all of the mulch and took it halfway across town. It was a great example of what incredible friends we have and how quickly they jumped in to help in whatever way they could.

Once the source of the water damage was identified, we needed to have the siding repaired. I reached out to my good friend Diane to ask if her son, who owns and operates a construction business, would have any recommendations. The next day, on a Saturday morning, two men showed up and tackled the siding repair. Within a couple of hours, they completed the job and went on their way.

A week later I called the office to find out who to pay for the work. I was told that one of the men who had done the repair work was a cancer survivor. Therefore, he was waving all charges for the work he and his son had done for us. I was so touched at the kindness and generosity from a complete stranger. It felt like cancer was providing us with an opportunity to see human beings at their very best, which was heartwarming *and humbling.*

---

**It felt like cancer was providing us with an opportunity to see human beings at their very best, which was heartwarming and humbling.**

---

• • • • • • • • • • •

# SCENE 9: SOME VERY BAD DAYS

Ten days later Ted started on the chemotherapy. We were very relieved that it involved oral chemo, rather than the type that would've been administered through an IV. He took eight *huge* pills every day, and then they'd scan him again in three months to determine the effectiveness of the treatment. Ideally, the chemo would shrink the tumors but with limited side-effects.

On April 22 of 2017, just three days after having started the chemo, Ted was outside doing some light yard work. All of a sudden he felt horrific pain in his gut. He fell to his hands and knees and soon crawled inside. He was writhing in pain, and I tried to ask him what was wrong, but he couldn't speak. I waited a minute as he crumpled to the floor of the family room, and as he continued to groan from the intense pain I realized we needed help — and fast!

I burst out our front door and ran to our neighbor's house. Thankfully, I found Tim Gutshall, our friend and doctor, outside working in his yard. Tim and I sprinted back to our house, and he came inside to assess Ted.

Within a few minutes he determined that Ted needed to get to the emergency room. Together, Tim and I got Ted up and into the car, and then I drove as fast as I could — yet he grimaced with every bump in the road, so I tried to also drive smoothly. I felt helpless and was worried something horrific might happen before we even got to the hospital. I'd never seen *anyone* in such pain, and it scared the heck out of me.

Once we arrived at the emergency room downtown, Ted was wheeled into an examining room fairly quickly. Within a few minutes, Tim showed up. His presence was calming, as I knew he was a man of deep faith and he'd also been an emergency doctor for many years.

By this point, due to the severity of the pain, Ted began to throw up. After being given several shots to settle his stomach, he continued to throw up. Tim literally held Ted's forehead and the bag as he continued to get sick. In the midst of a break, given that decades ago they'd been fraternity brothers, they joked that maybe this scene was a repeat from one of those days so long ago.

Once they got the nausea under control, they took some X-rays. Because it was a Saturday, we were told the radiologist who was on call would be visiting with us shortly. A few minutes later, in walked our friend, Dr. Bill Heggen, who just *happened* to be the senior radiologist on call that day and was already at the hospital. He went over the X-rays with us and then we waited for some additional tests to be run.

While waiting, Ted's heart monitor showed some stress, so they called the cardiologist on call. The doctor was *another* one of our friends, Dr. Jim Lovell. (Honestly, we don't know more than a handful of doctors and yet they were all present!) Jim was also a man of great faith, and therefore, when he came into the room, I felt additional relief.

Ted's pain finally began to respond to all the medications. At that time, the room was full of nurses, residents, Jim, Bill, Tim, me, and our son, John, who was 26 years old at that time. Jim, the heart doctor, asked for a moment of silence and spoke clearly and boldly; He prayed that God would provide exactly what Ted needed. I was touched by his demonstration of faith, and God's presence in the room was tangible.

Some might say we were lucky that three of the doctors were our friends. We knew better; those were all signs that God was with us and was orchestrating all the details.

The hospital was overcrowded so we remained in the emergency room for many hours, but finally later that night, they moved us to a room on the oncology floor. By that point I was *exhausted* and scared, and I fervently prayed this wouldn't become a major setback.

• • • • • • • • • • •

## SCENE 10: MY HOSPITAL AWAKENING

We soon learned that due to the cancerous tumors, the pancreas had stopped producing enough insulin. (THAT was what caused his blood sugar to be elevated!) As a result, Ted had become diabetic. That required having his blood sugar tested every few hours and then receiving insulin.

In addition, the neuroendocrine tumors produced excessive acid. That resulted in the formation of an ulcer in Ted's stomach. The horrific pain that had literally brought Ted to his knees was due to the ulcer bursting.

Usually, that'd require emergency surgery; however, given Ted's current condition, the trauma surgeon felt it was best to wait and see how his body responded over the next 12 to 24 hours.

He ended up avoiding surgery, but we weren't out of the woods just yet. Because of the tremendous stress his body was under, he began to have heart issues. Once again, our friend and cardiologist, Jim Lovell, came to the rescue — and he took care of not only Ted's heart, but also mine.

One day I was feeling particularly down. On my way out of the hospital to go home for a change of clothes, I ran into Jim and he could see I was struggling. He put his hand on my shoulder, looked me in the eyes and said, "Alicia, I believe in my heart that Ted is a miracle in progress." Because of his cardiology expertise and his deep faith, His words were extremely encouraging and provided the hope that I'd momentarily lost. Fortunately Ted's heart quickly returned to normal and we were both very grateful for Jim's care and kindness.

---

### "Alicia, I believe in my heart that Ted is a miracle in progress."

---

Unfortunately, Ted continued to lose weight (eventually, close to 40 pounds), and the following week he had to have a couple of blood transfusions. Ted was tired. I was tired. Fortunately God was not.

On April 30, 2017, we were *still* in the hospital and I was awakened in the middle of the night. That wasn't uncommon because the nurses had to check Ted's vitals every four hours, which made it challenging to sleep. But the nurses weren't the cause of my awakening. Instead, I felt this strong urge to pick up my Bible, which was on the floor next to my sleeping "bench." As I opened it specific passages seemed to jump off the page.

In Luke 17:11-19, Jesus told about His healing of ten lepers. I read that of the ten who received complete healing, only *one* returned to give thanks. The one who returned got on his knees and loudly praised Jesus.

As I pondered these verses, I felt God impress upon me that He was going to heal Ted. Not that He'd do so instantly, but that in time, He'd provide complete healing. In addition, I felt Him emphasize that we, Ted and I, would need to be bold about sharing the source of the healing and giving thanks to Him.

The next morning, after Ted woke up, I shared the scripture with him. He was still too weak to make much of a comment, but I tucked it in the back of my mind for future reference.

---

**"Now on his way to Jerusalem, Jesus traveled along the border between Samaria and Galilee. As he was going into a village, ten men who had leprosy met him. They stood at a distance and called out in a loud voice, 'Jesus, Master, have pity on us!' When he saw them, he said, 'Go show yourselves to the priests.' And as they went, they were cleansed. One of them when he saw he was healed, came back, praising God in a loud voice. He threw himself at Jesus' feet and thanked him — and he was a Samaritan. Jesus asked, 'Were not all ten cleansed? Where are the other nine? Has no one returned to give praise to God except this foreigner.' Then He said to him, 'Rise and go, your faith has made you well.'"**
**(Luke 17:11-19)**

---

One evening I finally accepted an invitation to get out of the hospital for a break. I met two of my best friends, Kelly and Denise, at a restaurant not too far from the hospital. I enjoyed having something other than hospital food, and they listened intently as I shared and processed all that had recently happened.

The outing was very therapeutic, but at the same time I felt bad for not being with Ted. Although my brother-in-law had graciously agreed to stay with Ted so that I could be relieved for a bit, I was more than anxious to get back to him.

When we'd made our mad dash to the emergency room on Saturday, we had no idea that we'd still be in the hospital six days later. And at that point there were no indications that we'd be released any time soon.

We were immensely thankful for my sister and several others who were so supportive; they handled our dog — a mini goldendoodle named Mabel, the mail, the yard, and anything else that was needed.

Family and friends wanted to come visit, but since Ted had been so weak I'd tried to keep that to a minimum. Even though I knew all the visitors meant well and didn't stay too long, their visits really wore him out.

After being in the hospital several more days I took another short break. I went home to have a bite of dinner, shower, and repack before heading back downtown. My friend Claudia picked up dinner and brought it over. It was a beautiful, warm evening, so we sat out on our deck while we talked and ate.

Claudia knew all too well what we were going through. Her husband, Brad, had been diagnosed with the more common and more deadly type of pancreatic cancer. Tragically, just three months after his diagnosis he passed away.

I hated that she'd had to go through the loss of her spouse. At the same time, it was a vivid example of how God uses people's experiences to encourage us in ways that others can't; some things are only understood by those who've gone through what you're going through.

Again, as much as I enjoyed the outing, I cut it short so I could get back to Ted as soon as possible. Although I'd long ago learned the importance of self-care, I was finding it more challenging while I was so focused on taking care of Ted. But I reminded myself that if I didn't take care of my own needs, I'd be much less helpful to Ted or anyone else.

The next week involved more ups and downs. It started with them having to put two drainage tubes into Ted's abdomen to support healing from the ruptured ulcer. Therefore, he was restricted to nothing but ice chips. Fortunately, he wasn't clamoring for anything more.

On day 12 in the hospital, we were thankful for great nurses, highly skilled doctors, and again, the outpouring of support from family, friends, and complete strangers. In addition, we were blessed by a visit and time of prayer by two people from our church; Pastor Jeremy and a friend Michael who is better known as Megs.

Ted had been dozing, and his mouth was extremely dry, making it rather difficult for him to talk. Therefore, as Jeremy and Megs prayed at the side of his hospital bed, Ted rested quietly with his eyes shut. After they finished praying, it was obvious he'd heard every word. Ted opened his eyes and voiced his own prayer with a stronger voice than I'd heard in weeks, which brought us all to tears.

---

**"Come to me, all who are weary and carry heavy burdens, and I will give you rest." (Matthew 11:28)**

---

The staff provided daily goals for Ted to accomplish; those included making several laps around the oncology floor with a walker, taking a shower, and having some time out on the patio in which to soak up the sun. All of that required plenty of napping in between, as he'd lost a lot of strength and stamina. The doctors continued to stress that the healing process was going to be very slow, and the importance of patience.

We continued to be hopeful that we'd be heading home soon, ideally early the next week.

After 17 days of sleeping on the vinyl bench at the hospital, I came home for the night. I needed a good night's sleep in my own bed. Ted had been doing much better, so he was fine with my leaving, and in fact had been encouraging me to do so for the past several days.

I waited to make sure Ted was almost asleep before I left, so when I got home it was already close to 9:00 P.M. Due to the water damage we'd experienced, our bedroom had to be repainted and the carpet replaced. Therefore, some of the furniture was still pushed to the middle of the room. I was exhausted and wanted nothing more than to fall into bed and fall asleep.

Instead, I pushed and pulled to reposition the furniture into its rightful place. When I'd finished, I plugged in our TV but couldn't get it to work. Since Mabel was staying at my sister's house, I felt very much alone and just wanted to have the sound from the TV to help me drift off to sleep. I tried resetting everything, and still it wouldn't work.

Frustrated and very weary, I sat on the bed and broke down. I sobbed and cried out to God, "This is hard, *really hard!* I feel so alone and right now I just need the TV to work. I know it's a small thing, but *please* help me." I got up and gave it one more try. This time, when I plugged it in, exactly as I had before, it worked! I let out a deep sigh, and said, "Thank You, Lord. That's all I need right now."

After sleeping like a log, I woke up, showered, and went right back downtown to the hospital. I was relieved to hear that Ted had also slept well.

Because of his becoming diabetic, we had to learn how to check his blood sugar and to do so several times every day. I usually wasn't queasy about things like that, but somehow that made me really anxious. I was also concerned about the lack of nursing care once we'd get back home. But both of us couldn't *wait* to get out of the hospital!

• • • • • • • • • • •

## SCENE 11: NO PLACE LIKE HOME

Nineteen days after arriving at the hospital, we were very *thankful* to be released and were getting settled back home. Sleeping in our own bed (along with our dog Mabel) was just one of the comforts of home that we greatly appreciated.

Both sides of our family brought us delicious home-cooked meals, which were a welcome relief from the hospital food. Actually, Ted had been living on "TNT" which was a liquid concoction that he'd received through an IV, so he was thrilled to be able to eat some normal food.

Also, because of the water damage in the main floor, and the resulting construction and repair, we dreaded walking into a mess. But our son's girlfriend, Jessi, was an interior designer. At her prompting, she and John had come over and put all the furniture back in place. In addition, Jessi pressed and hung the drapes and accessorized the room beautifully.

She later explained that she'd wanted our home to feel inviting when we walked back in the door. It was such a thoughtful and generous thing to do, which was just one example of her kind-hearted personality.

Over the next few weeks a medical service provided a nurse who came to our home every few days. She was wonderful, so encouraging and helpful in managing Ted's care. We grew to be comfortable testing his blood sugar, and within six weeks it had returned to normal. Therefore, blood sugar was something we no longer had to deal with. *That* was a relief!

Initially, our goal was for Ted to walk (with my assistance) just to the end of our driveway. Within a few weeks he extended his distance to walk to the end of our block and back, although sometimes even that was very challenging.

Throughout the following weeks we continued to pray fervently and to encourage one another with God's words from the Bible.

---

**"Don't worry about anything; instead, pray about everything. Tell God what you need, and thank Him for all he has done. Then you will experience God's peace, which exceeds anything we can understand. His peace will guard your hearts and minds as you live in Christ Jesus."**
**(Philippians 4:6-7)**

**"Cast your anxiety on him because he cares for you."**
**(1st Peter 5:7)**

---

In my journal that day, I recorded Matthew 7:11; "If you then, being evil, know how to give good gifts to your children, how much more will your Father who is in Heaven give good things to those who ask him!"

Several times a day, we prayed very specifically; we continued to ask and believe in God's complete healing of Ted's body. We reminded ourselves of the parting of the Red Sea and knew that nothing was impossible for God. We also knew God was still in the miracle business and believed the doctors would be speechless at the healing that would someday be evident in Ted, sooner rather than later.

I realized, for some, that sounded ridiculously optimistic or even naive. But based on a growing confidence through my prayer time, I believed that God was guiding us to pray and believe *wholeheartedly* for complete healing.

The message of James 1:6 made it clear; we can go to God with openness, boldness, and confidence. We can ask for what we want — what's in alignment with God's will, from the One who dispenses grace and mercy beyond what we could ever imagine.

---

"The apostles said to the Lord, 'Show us how to increase our faith.' The Lord answered, 'If you had faith even as small as a mustard seed, you could say to this mulberry tree, 'May you be uprooted and thrown into the sea,' and it would obey you!'"
(Luke 17:5-6)

"But when you ask, you must believe and not doubt, because the one who doubts is like a wave of the sea, blown and tossed by the wind."
(James 1:6)

---

• • • • • • • • • • •

# SCENE 12: POWERFUL GIFTS

In early June, a friend of our daughter's gave us a book. It was titled *Jehovah Rapha: The God Who Heals*, written by Mary J. Nelson. The book consisted of 72 healing prayers, with a Biblical story and accompanying scripture verses.

Within days of receiving it, I began reading it to Ted. It was so encouraging and comforting that it became a ritual of sorts. Each morning, I would apply Frankincense essential oil to his abdomen, and then placing my hand on him I'd declare the daily prayer out loud.

When I told friends what I was doing, they asked why I was using Frankincense. I'd been a big believer in using essential oils for quite a few years, but I'd also understood that Frankincense was one of the gifts the Three Wise Men gave to Mary. I'd said, "If it was good enough for Jesus, I figured it's good enough for Ted!" Truthfully, I believed it would be helpful to the healing process, and it felt comforting to use them along with our prayers — just to be clear: my faith was in God, not in the oils.

I was amazed at how often the daily entry in the book of healing prayers provided the exact words that were in my heart. Definitely a gift given at the perfect time, and a source of huge support and encouragement as we continued onward.

One particular morning, the daily devotional included a prayer (restated in my own words) that felt perfect for our current situation. "Father God, I know healing is no problem for you. Help me to have faith like the crippled man in the third and fourth chapters of Acts. Help me not to focus on my current circumstances, but rather, on your desire (and ability) to provide complete healing, for those who believe."

---

**"Through faith in the name of Jesus, this man was healed — and you know how crippled he was before. Faith in Jesus' name has healed him before your very eyes."**
**(Acts 3:16)**

---

We continued to be so thankful for God's provision. Ted hadn't had any side effects, had been gaining strength, and was able to walk farther each day. He was still struggling to gain weight, but we knew it would be a slow process. (I kept thinking how great it would be if we could donate weight to him, like donating blood.)

We continued to be thankful that he'd had no nausea, which was the most common side effect of the chemo drugs. We were also thankful that his appetite had picked up (especially given his significant weight loss) and his digestive system had settled down.

June 7, 2017, we had another oncology appointment, and Dr. Buroker gave us the perspective that we'd been praying for. He explained that a chromogranin number indicates the strength and activity of the tumors. He said that while he'd have been happy with a drop of 500 points within the month, Ted's had dropped 8,000! In his words, "We're hitting this out of the ballpark!" We were thrilled and very thankful for the blessings from God. It was a great way to start the Father's Day weekend.

> **"Good news is like cold water to a weary soul."**
> **(Proverbs 25:25)**

June 10, 2017 was a fabulous day! We were able to surprise everybody in our extended families with the surprise of our son's engagement.

We had everyone over for what they *thought* was a typical Father's Day brunch. Ted's employer had wanted to do something in the way of providing meals for us, so they generously provided the food for our brunch that day.

As planned, John and Jessi arrived about 10 minutes after everyone else was already enjoying mimosas and chatting. They burst into the kitchen, and John said in his booming voice, "I'd like to introduce you to my fiancée, Jessi!" Everyone went crazy with loud hoots and hollers of surprise!

A few minutes later, as a surprise to Jessi, her mom and dad arrived. It was so great that they made the four-hour drive to join the festivities, and I knew it meant the world to Jessi to have them there.

Once they caught their breath, John and Jessi gave a detailed account of how he had proposed the evening before. It was so fun to hear them both chime in, adding their own version of the story.

We had such peace of mind, believing they were made for each other. Also, it felt great to focus on something positive and joyful in the midst of such uncertainty about Ted's health and the road that might be in front of us.

Ted was still painfully thin and had very limited stamina, but he managed to rally. Although everyone was a little anxious about his condition, having him participate was encouraging and it made the celebration even more memorable.

> **Psalm 118:24 says, "This is the day the Lord has made;**
> **let us rejoice and be glad in it."**

At our next month's appointment, Dr. Buroker told us *not* to expect as much of a drop in the chromogranin number as that of the previous month. He explained that the reduction typically slows way down after the initial treatment. Nonetheless, we got the news that the number dropped again, to 1,600! That was more than a 75 percent reduction!. As Ted's brother, Steve, said, "Those last 1,600 don't stand a chance!"

A month later, on July 12, I woke up with a very clear thought impressed upon my mind. As I prayed and asked God to confirm it, he showed me that it was time for Ted to take over the healing prayers for himself. Initially, he'd been too weak to do so, but over the past month he'd become stronger.

So I went downstairs and found him reading the newspaper. I explained what I'd felt God was asking us to do, and he agreed that he could now do that.

Later that morning, I went to a local Panera Bread, where I was hosting a small gathering; it was an information coffee for Wholehearted Living. During these gatherings I talk about how the program was established in 2010, the approach we take to help women connect with the wounds of their past, and the importance of learning to become their own greatest fan — rather than continuing to be their biggest critic. I also go through the details of each of the three eight-week courses: Your Relationship with Yourself, Your Relationship with Cravings and Your Relationship with God.

These gatherings provide an opportunity for women to decide if they are just interested or are truly *committed* to doing the decluttering work that is involved. For that very reason, I stress the importance of showing up for the weekly small group coaching sessions with their assignment completed to the very best of their ability, without any excuses. I also explain that their growth is not only for themselves as it will actually have a big impact on the others in the coaching group — and vice versa.

For those that are committed, the next step is to determine if they would be a good match for the available openings we have. I try to match clients who I think would have some things in common with each other and have similar availability. However, the placement for new clients is something I don't take lightly and so I always pray, asking God for *His* guidance for each one.

That particular day, just as the gathering was coming to an end, an acquaintance of mine walked in. As the other women were leaving she approached and asked me if I had a few minutes to talk, so I sat back down.

I knew this woman only through our daughter and her son having been part of the same high school performing group. She began by telling me she had something she needed to tell me. (*That* certainly got my attention!)

She then asked me if I was familiar with spiritual gifts and in particular prophetic visions or dreams. I shared that I was, and in fact I'd researched and written a chapter about them in one of my previous books.

She went on to tell me that ever since she'd been a little girl she'd had prophetic visions. She shared several examples of what that'd involved, and I listened intently.

She then shared that ever since she'd heard of Ted's diagnosis of stage four pancreatic cancer, she'd had a crystal clear vision — not just once, but several times. Each time, she said the vision was of Ted as an old grandpa. He was in a park with our daughter, Kristin, and several grandchildren playing at his feet.

She asked me if that resonated with me for any reason, and I had goosebumps as I shared that when Ted was first diagnosed, my heart's cry was for God not to deny him the joy of being a grandfather. I couldn't imagine anyone being a better, more loving grandfather to our children's children, and knowing how important that was to him, it hit me hard.

Therefore, the fact that she explicitly mentioned him being a grandfather was deeply encouraging to me. She then hesitated for just a second, and then told me there was one more thing that God had impressed upon her as she'd been praying earlier that morning.

She said, "I don't understand the significance of this, but He showed me that it's important for Ted to take over praying for the healing of his own body." I nearly fell off my chair! I quickly explained my experience from earlier that morning, and we both marveled at God's incredible provision.

After we finished talking I drove back home. On my way, as I was audibly thanking God for the gift of confirmation and encouragement, tears were streaming down my face. I'm not sure I'd ever felt God's presence any stronger than at that moment. I felt deeply cared for by Him and was confident He'd provide whatever we needed in the months and years ahead.

Upon arriving, I shared the experience with Ted. He, too, was brought to tears. I went to get the book of Biblical stories, and he immediately read one out loud and then boldly declared the companion healing prayer. We both wept and didn't say a word; we didn't need to. We hugged one another and just sat in stillness for several minutes.

· · · · · · · · · · · ·

# SCENE 13: HITTING A HOMERUN

In August 2017, we met with Dr. Buroker for Ted's monthly oncology appointment. Tom said, "If you'd have asked me back in April what hitting a homerun would look like, *this is it!* Ted's blood work looks as good as yours or mine!"

We were ecstatic to hear his words! There was nothing better than thinking of the day when the doctors would look at the scans, and would be speechless, seeing no evidence of any cancer in Ted's body! We knew when that happened, we'd know who to thank for such miraculous results.

The largest tumors had been five inches long and had shrunk to less than two! We had no doubt that God was providing miraculous healing, and that Ted would live a long and purposeful life.

We received the chromogranin number the following morning, and although we were told not to expect a drop as significant as the previous month, it dropped another 45 percent (from 587 to 325)!

Two months later, on October 27, we hosted John and Jessi's rehearsal dinner. It may have been one of the best days of my life. Honestly, I don't think it could have gone any better! From the venue, the back room of a Jazz Club, Noce, to the table settings, the food, the pianist, the jazz ensemble, and the speeches, it couldn't have been more beautiful and enjoyable.

Deeply meaningful was the honor and glory that the evening gave to

God. Ted's speech included that there was no better foundation on which to build a marriage or do anything, than on their relationship with God. Then John said that everyone in the room had two things in common: first, that no matter what their political or spiritual beliefs may be, we were all made in the image of Jesus Christ, and, second, that they knew either Jessi or John.

I shared that for many years I'd specifically prayed for the future spouse for our kids, and the night we'd met Jessi I said to Ted, "*That* is who we've been praying for. Jessi is who John's going to marry," to which Ted replied, "I think you're right."

I enjoyed teaching the most basic 12-step Greek dance to all those who were adventurous enough to try it. Then nearly everyone, close to 60 people, joined hands and formed a large circle to give it a try. It felt magical to look around the room and see people that we loved so deeply dancing and having so much fun together.

Later in the evening, many people stepped up to the microphone and spoke, including Jackie, one of my nieces. She said, "Although I'm not Greek by blood, I'm Greek by *love!*" Julianne, my other niece, said how much she and John had grown up being forced to spend time together because they were cousins and very close in age. In contrast, she shared that as adults they'd become good friends and did things together by choice.

Initially, I'd thought we'd make the evening an early night, since the wedding festivities would start so early the following day. But after the dinner, the speeches, and the Greek dancing, John pumped his latest playlist over the sound system and our entire family and a few good friends continued to dance. Close to midnight I realized it was *only* our family that was still dancing — and we were all going strong; we laughed, danced, and enjoyed each other in ways that felt especially meaningful given the challenges we'd been facing.

As if that wasn't enough, once we got back home, we stayed up for another hour talking in the kitchen with our best friends, the Keslers, who were staying with us. We relived every aspect of the evening and laughed 'til I thought we'd pee our pants! It was a blast and the perfect ending to a perfect day. Honestly, I wondered how the wedding could top that, but I was hopeful it would.

As I went to bed that night I felt my heart would burst if I'd been any happier. Yet at the same time, from all the dancing I'd done, my feet felt like someone had beaten them with a baseball bat!

The next evening, John and Jessi were married. It was a beautiful ceremony at a brand-new event center, The Des Moines Tea Room. Jessi was a stunning bride, and John looked equally handsome. When he got his first look at her, the expression on his face said it all; without a doubt we'd never seen him any happier.

The reception was a lot of fun and again, everyone participated in a Greek dance. It was really cool to see several hundred people arm in arm, in one giant circle that reached the outer walls of the ballroom. People seemed to enjoy the heck out of something that was new and different for most of them. As I soaked it all up, I was keenly aware of the love God had for each of us and the faith that He'd developed in our family and friends. And I went to bed that night with a very grateful heart.

November 16 we met with Dr. Buroker. We were thrilled to hear the news, that the tumors in the liver were in remission. Therefore, we'd be heading to Iowa City the first of the year to talk about next steps.

There had been some talk about the possibility of Ted having surgery, in which they'd remove the portion of the pancreas that was the original source of the cancer. In addition, we'd lightly talked about the possibility of them also removing a portion of Ted's liver. We were fascinated to learn that the liver is the only organ in the body that will regenerate itself, meaning that you can remove up to half of the liver and it will regrow into a full-sized, fully functioning liver.

We were continuing to learn the cancer diagnosis was the biggest gift we'd been given; we realized the cancer diagnosis was helping us learn to walk by faith and not by sight.

---

**"For we live by faith and not by sight." (2nd Corinthians 5:7)**

---

I had no idea what the future held, but I was confident who held it. So for the time being, I just prayed for clarity and confirmation for the right medical decisions to move ahead.

## 2018

On January 3, 2018, we drove to Iowa City and met with another oncologist who'd been participating in overseeing Ted's care. He was happy to hear that Ted was feeling well, going to the gym four days a week, and working full-time and admittedly hadn't felt this great in years. Ted's scans and blood counts all showed everything was stable, and obviously he had been responding to the chemo very well.

We'd been hoping to hear that they could do surgery or freeze or radiate the last of the tumors in Ted's liver. We were both really disappointed to hear that neither of those were options. The doctor went on to say that Ted was doing so well that we should continue with the same oral chemo that he'd been taking the past eight months. He said, "Why rock the boat when you're doing so well?"

On our drive back home, Ted said that he was disappointed, but at the same time he saw it as a gift; he shared that especially at the start of a new year, it was good to be reminded of our complete and total reliance on God for everything. I about fell out of the car realizing just how deep Ted's faith had become.

The crazy thing is that the morning after our Iowa City appointment, I awoke with a vivid picture in my mind. I told Ted that I realized we're all dancing with death, it's just that now Ted's dance partner had a name, "pancreatic cancer." Naming it somehow made it feel more present and imminent, but that wasn't necessarily true. I could be run over by a bus that very day! I shared that with Ted, and he felt my belief was reassuring.

---

**"For I hold you by your right hand — I, the Lord your God.
And I say to you, 'Don't be afraid. I am here to help you.'"
(Isaiah 41:13 NLT)**

---

For the past eight years since its inception, I had done everything I could to operate and expand the Wholehearted Living business. With a growing number of clients I realized the need to recruit and train additional heart coaches. So I developed a training program, established criteria to become certified and (eventually with some help) trained nine heart coaches for new Wholehearted Living clients. At the same time, I was continually making improvements to the curriculum and further developing the exercises so they were even more effective in helping women apply what they learned in the program.

I also developed and recorded teaching videos for each of the 25 weekly sessions, created additional tools like cheat sheets, a letter writing overview and a collection of analogies to drive home the components of living wholeheartedly. *Everything* I created was to help clients develop a healthier relationship with themselves — with God and with other people too.

In addition to all of that, I handled our marketing, accounting and all the logistics for the business. I managed our website, our social media and wrote our weekly "tip for living wholeheartedly," semi-monthly blogs and more. Much of those responsibilities were new to me so I had to learn a lot of things by trial and error. Fortunately that helped me to become less critical of myself when I made mistakes, which contributed to my own growth. I learned to give myself grace just like I so easily do for my friends or others.

Throughout those eight years I was invigorated by the hard work it required. I was energized by seeing the results clients were experiencing and how many of the heart coaches were continuing to grow and develop, and I thrived on creating new content — even though that took *months* of intense work. I was also constantly learning, researching and taking classes or attending training seminars, so I could become better equipped to develop the business. But there were also numerous times where I wondered why in the heck I didn't just give up and close the doors.

One Sunday morning, during a time of feeling particularly discouraged, I decided to have someone pray for me after our church service. The woman looked close to my age and had a friendly smile, so I stepped over to her and asked her to pray for me. I introduced myself with only my first name, Alicia, and told her I needed some encouragement, but I said nothing else. She was a total stranger to me, and yet when she closed her eyes and began praying, her words about knocked me off the platform!

She shared that God was showing her a vivid picture of me; she said I was wearing shoes that sparkled, and the light that shone so brightly from them was almost blinding. Then she said that with every step I took, the light was being shared and that lives were being changed in the process. She went on to share that God had big plans for me and that He wanted me to share His message.

When she finished, I told her about Wholehearted Living and about my husband's cancer. She said she'd like to stay connected to hear about Ted's progress, so I gave her my full name and email. In return, she introduced herself by her full name. Are you ready for this? She was the wife of the physician who'd initially put Ted on the diabetic medicine and hadn't run additional tests!

Since Ted's diagnosis, I'd thought about the fact that *had* more tests been done, they'd have caught the pancreatic cancer almost eight or nine months earlier. But since then, I'd forgiven the doctor for not doing the additional testing. I'd figured that insurance companies likely discouraged doctors from running tests that were expensive and might prove to be unnecessary. In addition, we all make mistakes and his certainly hadn't been intentional.

I went home and spent a good hour or more journaling, praying, and reflecting on the words of encouragement God had provided. I also marveled at how God uses things we think of as bad for a much greater good.

In addition, I reflected upon the tremendous blessings of the the past months. I thought of how Tim Gutshall (our friend, neighbor and doctor) had so often helped us to understand the medical terminology, to navigate insurance claims, and prayed for us and encouraged us.

I thought of Bill Heggen (our friend and radiologist) who called us each time as soon as possible with the results of Ted's latest scans. Also how he and his wife, Lynn, had taken us out for dinner and even brought over some of his homemade chocolate fudge sauce — and it was *delicious*!

I thought of Nancy Bell (my previous neighbor while growing up) who had spent a lot of time on the phone with me; she became like a mother to me and was a tremendous source of comfort. Given her deep faith, her prayers and words of wisdom often provided exactly what I needed. And there were so many others who'd provided meals and sent texts, emails or cards. They were all examples of God's flawless provision through the generosity and kindness of others.

• • • • • • • • • • •

# SCENE 14: STAGE ZERO

On January 15, 2018, I went in for my routine mammogram and was called back for some additional views. No big deal; they assured me that this was quite common, and that the vast majority of the time there's nothing more that would need to be done.

A week later I went back for more views. I was called the next day with the news. The doctor had seen something that was concerning and the breast would, therefore, require a needle biopsy.

The day after I had the biopsy, I was at home waiting for the doctor's call. I said out loud, "God, I have a feeling that there's more you want to do in this healing journey, so if I'm to be part of this, then bring it on. I want whatever is necessary to draw others to come to know You."

Literally minutes later the phone rang. It was the doctor. She shared that I had breast cancer, officially, "inductile carcinoma, stage zero." I wasn't at all surprised or worried about my diagnosis. After all, I was confident God was active in the midst of my life, and stage zero sounded harmless.

After many additional mammogram views, a needle biopsy, an MRI, and then an ultrasound, they determined there were several other areas of *potential* concern. So they did two more needle biopsies the following week.

During many of these appointments people inquired about my peace, so I was able to talk about the source of my peace — which was God. And I had no doubt He was using my cancer for a bigger purpose.

Once again, I marveled at God's provision. Not at all a coincidence that right after Christmas I felt led to organize and document every last detail that anyone would need to present our current Wholehearted Living workshops. So I did. Then, despite my upcoming surgeries and time off my team had everything they would need to present these without me.

Best of all, we saw provision for Kristin. She was accepted and went through an interview for a job at Drake University, which sounded ideal for her. I prayed that she'd get the job if it was God's will and if so, that she'd find a place to live.

With all that was on my heart I continued to trust God was actively at work in all areas. I had no idea what the future held, but I was confident who held it. Therefore, I prayed for wisdom to make the best medical decisions, trusting God would lead me to those.

After several biopsies and additional mammograms and an MRI, I was presented with two options: one was to have a simple lumpectomy, followed by 16 radiation treatments and then five years on an anti-cancer drug. The second option would involve a pretty drastic surgery (a bilateral mastectomy). I was torn about the right decision so talked it over with Ted, several doctors, friends, and of course prayed about it. Realizing that God created every single cell of my body, I felt a peace that He knew exactly what was best for me, and I received confirmation in my gut.

Dr. Buroker readily agreed to be my oncologist, which was great — though I'd never thought Ted and I would share a cancer doctor! Unfortunately, it wasn't too much longer before my good friend Lynn was also diagnosed with breast cancer; Dr. Buroker was her oncologist as well. One of the high points of our friendly coffee and therapy sessions together, was recanting Dr. Buroker's hilarious comments and all the ways he helped us get through our cancers.

We also got a wonderful answer to our prayers for Kristin; she'd been offered and had accepted the job at Drake. Because she had to finish up with some big commitments in Minneapolis, Ted and I, along with my sister, picked out an apartment for her. Talk about trusting your people! Of course, we Face Timed and showed it to her the best we could. She'd be moving to Des Moines on May 5, just in time for my breast cancer surgery five days later. Obviously, another example of God's perfect provision.

On May 10 Dr. Lekkas and Dr. Hamling collaborated for surgery; one handled the mastectomy while the other completed the first phase of the reconstruction process; that involved putting in tissue expanders to make room for breast implants that would be put in at another time. The surgery went smoothly and required just an overnight stay in the hospital. The next morning, by the time the post-op team made their rounds,

I was dressed and ready to leave for home. People were surprised that my recovery was so quick, but I felt like this was nothing more than a bump in the road — actually two bumps in the road.

My decision to go ahead with the double mastectomy proved to be a good thing — actually it proved to be a *God thing!* The post-pathology report showed that I had multiple cancerous spots, throughout *both* breasts! Also, because the quick-freeze pathology during the surgery had shown no further signs of cancerous tissue, they left a small portion behind (to help with the reconstruction process). But the post-surgery report four or five days later, showed there was cancer in the remaining tissue. There was also a spot on the lining of my pectoral muscle, so *another* surgery would be required to scrape that area. Because of the reconstruction process, we decided to wait several months and combine that with the next scheduled procedure.

One of the many blessings throughout my cancer experiences was meeting outstanding people like Shari Houston, the nurse at Dr. Lekkas' office. Right from the first appointment Shari made me feel like she was my best friend and that she would be taking each step of this journey with me. She was extremely compassionate and kind, patient with all of my questions, and even supported me with her prayers. Several of my friends had told me how amazing she had been for each of them, and I soon realized they hadn't exaggerated one bit!

Throughout the summer and early fall Ted's chemotherapy had to be changed several times. The types he'd been receiving weren't shrinking the tumors like we'd hoped and newer versions seemed more promising. However the newer treatments required him to go to the lab for the chemo to be provided through an IV. After 48 hours he'd have to go back to the lab to have it unhooked, only to repeat that two weeks later. It got to be an inconvenience, but it really didn't make him feel much different, so it didn't interfere with most of the things he wanted to do.

He'd often leave the chemo lab and go directly to work. Since he worked at a bank and wore a suit every day, it was easy to hide the apparatus beneath his suit jacket, so it wasn't obvious.

With Ted's Greek skin and head of thick, silver hair, he was as handsome as ever, and people who knew about his cancer would often ask us if the doctors had made a mistake; they indicated that he looked way too healthy to have stage four pancreatic cancer. I had to agree.

In the past, on the side, Ted had occasionally done some modeling for TV commercials, magazines, and other publications. In the midst of stage four pancreatic cancer, his agent called and told him he'd been chosen to be featured in an upcoming TV ad. In it, they had Ted sitting on a sandy beach relaxing in a Hawaiian shirt and shorts. When he came home from the photo shoot, we both commented that the crew probably wouldn't have believed it had he told them about his cancer. It really was hard to believe.

In October we went back to Mayo for a new scan and it revealed disappointing results from the most recent chemo treatments. So after discussing the options with Dr. Thor, we agreed to a brand new type of treatment called PRRT. It was a molecular therapy that would send chemo directly to the tumors with matching receptors, and then release high doses of radiation inside them. They scheduled four treatments — one every other month — and explained that they'd be administered through full day sessions at Mayo hospital. Each treatment would require a strict protocol, having the entire room taped off and sanitized with access to no one but trained staff wearing protective gear. It sounded scary but again, our hopes were high that this would be the answer.

In November 2018 I had my second surgery. The doctors removed the small amount of breast tissue, replaced the tissue expanders with the implants, and were able to scrape the lining of the pectoral wall to get clean margins.

Throughout my first two surgeries, in additional to being extremely attentive to me, Ted was able to maintain his normal schedule. He worked full-time, exercised several days a week, cooked meals, shoveled snow and handled household projects too. He managed to do everything he'd always done and didn't miss a beat.

## 2019

In mid-January of 2019, I had my third surgery, and it looked like it'd be my last. However, an issue developed with the healing. In addition new reports had come out that the type of implant they'd used in my reconstruction surgery, was now associated with an elevated risk of developing lymphoma. (I had gone through all of this so as to reduce my chances of having another cancer. So obviously, I was extremely bummed to hear that news.)

Throughout the winter and early spring, we made the repeated trips to Mayo for Ted's PRRT treatments. Each one heightened my anxiety about the toxicity of what was being put into his body, but I was also very relieved that he was not having any adverse side effects.

It was almost comical that I would make the four-hour drive back home with Ted sitting in the back seat, as far away from me as possible; he had to be more than six feet away from me or anyone else since he was still considered to be radioactive. (He told me he had a new appreciation for what it would have felt like to be a leper in Jesus' day.) In addition it involved many changes at home for the next week. He had to sleep in a different bedroom, use only one bathroom, and even his laundry had to be separated from my own. Truly more things than you can imagine had to be dealt with after each of those treatments.

June 13 I had my fourth breast cancer surgery. Dr. Lekkas fixed the healing issue and also switched out the implants. Everything went smoothly and he said that it should be the last one that'd be required. (I'd heard *that* before, so I was a bit leery.)

It'd been a year and a half since I'd been diagnosed with breast cancer and though it was initially categorized as "stage zero," four surgeries and 18 months later had felt like a *long* time! Yet more than anything, it'd been a major inconvenience and not much more than that. I felt a peace that allowed me to feel hopeful and happy, even in the midst of the more painful parts of my recovery.

•••••••••••

## SCENE 15: ACTIVE ADVENTURES

Mid July of 2019, Ted and I rode a day of RAGBRAI (an annual week-long bike ride across the state of Iowa). We covered 46 miles that day and although some of the hills were challenging, we conquered all of them. It felt great, and I was so glad that neither pancreatic cancer nor breast cancer could keep us from that experience.

The following day we drove back to Mayo. Unfortunately, the results were disappointing. Despite the four radioactive treatments, the tumors in the liver hadn't shrunk. In fact, the biggest ones had grown a fair amount. After discussing various options, we were all in agreement to return to the IV chemotherapy to try and knock the tumors back down.

Over the following few weeks I found myself revisiting my disappointment of the recent news, while also reviving my hope for the new approach. Consequently, I found myself thinking about healthy ways to handle the emotional roller coaster I'd been on for far too long.

In addition, after being officially declared cancer free, I decided I wanted to get back to running, which I had enjoyed in the past. Since I am motivated by setting fairly big goals, I chose to register for the Des Moines half marathon. The race would be held on October 20, 2019, which would be the day before my 60th birthday. I liked the thought of entering the next decade of life by feeling strong and healthy and achieving a lofty goal. And I also thought it would be a great way to raise money for a cause that was near and dear to my heart — the Charlie Cutler Healing and Wellness Endowment.

However, since it'd only been six weeks since my last surgery, I was still under doctor's orders not to exercise just yet. I was hopeful that I'd be released soon and could start walking and then eventually, running again.

I had to admit I was a little fearful and wondered if I could really run that far, as I'd never run more than two or three miles. At the same time, it sounded like a great goal, and I figured it'd be a lot of fun to accomplish.

My "jump in and the net will appear" approach to life has its advantages and disadvantages. I was released to start walking that same week and I wasted no time. I walked nearly every day, each time a bit farther than the day before.

After increasing my walking distance, I began to run and walk intermittently. Finally, on August 26, I was able to run four miles without stopping. It wasn't all that far but it sure felt good. I was reminded how out of shape I was, but was optimistic that I could gain some ground and feel good enough to run the half-marathon.

I'd recently found out that there was a 10-mile race in Des Moines the first Sunday in October. I figured that'd be a great test to see if I could make it that far, plus it would help me to keep training for the half-marathon, which would be just two weeks after that.

I found a training program to help me reach that kind of mileage, but I have to admit, the thought of running for a solid two hours or more seemed a bit crazy — *even to me!*

On September 12 I completed a 7-mile run. As I ran, I poured my heart out to God. I asked Him to provide what we needed. I was weary. Not only from managing Ted's cancer but also from additional challenges with growing the Wholehearted Living business.

I no sooner asked for encouragement than I turned the corner of the bike path and there, in the middle of the creek, was a deer lying down and looking straight at me. I stopped and was overcome with tears. God's provision felt like being wrapped up in a heavy fleece blanket while sitting next to a roaring fire. I eventually gathered myself and returned to my run. I ended up doing a second lap on the bike trail and again, the deer was *still* there. It was yet another vivid example of God's perfect timing.

September 15, 2019, I ran the Des Moines Capital Pursuit Race. I was a little nervous but also strongly believed I could finish the full 10-mile course. Even though I'd been training outside in hot weather, I'd never run in a lot of humidity. That morning included record breaking humidity and at 7:00 A.M. when the race started, it was already *really* hot! As I passed by Kristin and Ted who were cheering me on, I yelled, "So far, so good!" They laughed because at that point I'd only run about 20 steps.

Not yet into the third mile, I began to have significant pain in my right heel. I thought I'd probably end up with a little plantar fasciitis after the race, but certainly wasn't going to let anything stop me from crossing the finish line.

But the more I ran the more painful it became, and so I had no choice but to stop and walk. Yet even walking was soon very painful. In addition to my ailments, was the fact that I'd become dehydrated, and my blood sugar had dropped quite a bit.

Because I was an inexperienced long-distance runner, I was concerned about drinking water and then having to stop and go to the bathroom during the race. So to avoid having to do so, I'd only grabbed a tiny sip at one or two of the water stations. My approach, along with the high humidity, was a bad combination! I began to feel light-headed, like my legs were rubber, and I wasn't thinking clearly. Yet I'm a determined "old broad" and can push myself pretty hard, so I continued intermittently running and walking.

By the time I stumbled across the finish line, after three solid hours of running and walking in the intense heat and humidity, I couldn't even stand up by myself. Kristin and Ted quickly grabbed me, sat me down, got me a couple of bananas and several glasses of water. Then, after resting a bit, they drove me home. I showered and fell into bed for a two-hour nap.

When I woke up, I couldn't walk. I was unable to put *any* weight on my right foot! A visit to the orthopedic surgeon prompted a diagnosis of a stress fracture in my heel. I was put in a walking boot with two crutches and told, in no uncertain terms, that there was no way I could even *walk* the Des Moines half-marathon. I was extremely disappointed, as I'd *really* wanted to run the half-marathon.

One of the most valuable things I've learned (and that I stress to every-one I know) is the importance of validating feelings, whether our own or those of others. Validating feelings just means to give permission to *feel* the feelings.

While sharing my disappointing news (about not running the race), It was a huge source of comfort to have people validate my feelings rather than trying to fix them or to cheer me up. The following are a few that were most helpful:

"That stinks! Of course you'd be devastated, as this wasn't what you had trained so hard for. I'm so sorry."

Another shared, "You have every reason to be extremely bummed. I know how much this goal meant to you."

Even though I knew everyone had nothing but the best of intentions, some people responded with comments that weren't helpful, like, "Well, there's always next year," or "At least you were able to run the10-mile race. For me that's just as incredible as running a half marathon."

(When anyone starts with "at least," you can rest assured they are *not* going to validate your feelings. Instead, that's minimizing them, and that is anything *but* helpful.)

Validating feelings is one of the greatest gifts you can give yourself and others — and it'll cost you nothing. Plus, it'll always be a good fit.

---

**Validating feelings is one of the greatest gifts you can give yourself and others — and it'll cost you nothing. Plus, it'll always be a good fit.**

---

· · · · · · · · · · ·

# SCENE 16: ENCOURAGEMENT

November 13, 2019, we hosted our annual Wholehearted Living alum celebration. Each year as we had more women complete the three courses we decided to establish an annual event to acknowledge their accomplishment and to celebrate their transformation.

A couple of years ago one of my best friends had made a huge tree of brown felt that represented the Wholehearted Living family. The branches of the tree held a leaf for each of the women who'd graduated from our program. That evening we added 21 new leaves to our family tree.

I was grateful for the team that had helped to make it all possible; first, God, then the board members, coaches, and all the clients. It was uplifting to think about the fact that Wholehearted Living started in 2010 with just three women around my kitchen table, and at that point we had close to 200 graduates.

At the end of the evening, we stood in a large circle and each one shared what they'd gotten out of the courses. I was humbled and in awe as I heard of the "good fruit" that God has produced through Wholehearted Living.

Many shared that it saved or greatly improved their marriage. Others said it helped them to leave an abusive, toxic relationship, or that they gained the tools to grieve family wounds and then deal with the loss of a parent, meaningful job, or other relationship.

Others shared how they learned how to take care of themselves instead of taking care of everyone else at their own expense, how to say "no" without feeling guilty, and how to establish healthy boundaries in many areas of their lives.

The *most* meaningful testimonies were from those who said it facilitated their development of a deeper, more vibrant relationship with God. *That's* my greatest hope for anyone, whether in the program or not.

The next morning in my quiet time with God, He led me to John 15:2. It says, "He cuts off every branch in me that bears no fruit, while every branch that does bear fruit He prunes so that it will be even more fruitful." He impressed upon me that He intended to prune the tree of Wholehearted Living, for the sole purpose of producing greater fruit.

Although at one time we'd had up to 12 women on the Wholehearted Living team, as mentioned before, many had moved on to other seasons of their lives. Throughout the next week or so, God also showed me that I was to "expand my tent," as together, we'd be reaching many more women with the Wholehearted Living curriculum.

Logically, this made no sense. How were we going to reach *more* women with fewer team members? Fortunately, I'd come to understand that God's ways are higher than mine, and I was confident that He would reveal His plan and provision as He saw fit.

Late in the fall, I attended an all-day workshop on improving your prayer life. It was very powerful, and I came home with a renewed commitment to find a specific time and place in which to pray; I wanted to be more intentional about connecting with God. I got to work and cleaned out a spare bedroom for that very purpose.

Over the next several days, I started a new ritual; every morning I'd make a cup of my favorite hot spiced tea, get a protein bar, and settle into my comfy chair. I'd quiet myself in preparation, and then pray, thanking God for His presence.

In the Wholehearted Living program, I teach women to share their heart with God; to share anything they're thinking, feeling, wanting, or needing. Also to share their praises and thanksgiving, and anything else they have on their mind. I instruct them to do that in the form of a letter; they write a letter to God and sign it from their heart.

Then I teach them to sit quietly and ask God what He wants to share in response. For some — actually for most women — this takes them out of their comfort zone. They're afraid they'll not hear from Him, or they feel it's presumptuous of them to be able to write what God would want to say.

I often share that growth only happens when we're willing to leave our comfort zone. When you actually think about it, oftentimes, our comfort zones aren't all that comfortable. If you truly desire a closer, more vibrant relationship with Christ, then remaining stuck with a dull prayer life isn't really comfortable!

Thinking it's presumptuous to be able to write down God's response indicates the belief that God doesn't want us to know His will — and nothing could be further from the truth.

Imagine sharing your heart with a loving, protective, kind and compassionate father, and then asking what He thinks. Can you imagine him being silent or making it difficult to understand what he wants to share? Of course not!

It's the same with God. He likes you. He loves you. He yearns for times of deep connections with you and wants you to get to know Him better. To do so, He doesn't intend to make it difficult or some kind of a game.

Instead, His Word says that His sheep hear His voice. So as I prepared myself each morning to write my letter to God, and then write my perception of His response, I reminded myself that He knew my mind wandered. He knew that even after writing those types of letters for over a decade, that in the midst of writing them I still questioned whether the words were His rather than my own. I came to understand, however, that He was big enough to get through to me.

I often felt reassured with the belief that anything I faced wasn't a surprise to God, nor was it a problem. He was more than capable of providing exactly what I needed, at exactly the right time. My job was to have faith and to live with peace and joy in the midst of my circumstances.

---

**"Faith is the confidence that what we hope for will actually happen; it gives us the assurance of things we cannot see."**
**(Hebrews 11:1)**

**"Looking straight at him, Paul realized he had faith to be healed. So Paul called to him in a loud voice, 'Stand up!' And the man jumped to his feet and started walking."**
**(Acts 14:9-10)**

---

· · · · · · · · · · ·

# SCENE 17: THE RELEVANCE OF A NAME

The weeks before Thanksgiving, 2019, I felt God nudging me to expand Wholehearted Living to reach more women, and to do so by branding my name. Initially I really fought the idea because I knew the work I did was not about me — it was about God and the transforming work that *He* does through the Wholehearted Living curriculum. But this is what then transpired:

When I'd begun to journal to God about this topic, He brought several things to my attention. First, that Beth Moore's ministry was branded under her name, it's Beth Moore with Lifeway Ministries. Also, that she doesn't point people to *her*, but rather to God, the same as my heart's greatest desire.

Second, the tools He provided to me were to help women claim their true *identity*, and yet I'd not been using my own. (That hit me kind of like a "V-8 moment!") Also, I reflected upon the fact that I'd felt like a misfit most of my life — I'd grown up unable to find my name on anything, which only confirmed that I didn't fit in. Now I was learning to claim my uniqueness, including my less than normal name.

Lastly, God led me to a reading in my devotional that explained His name,

"Emmanuel," means "God with us." He then reminded me of something I'd learned years ago; a man who my employer was hosting from Israel taught me that in Hebrew, the meaning of "Alicia" was "God's truth."

I started to believe God had named me exactly as He desired. At that point I no longer lamented over the fact that my first and last names wouldn't exactly roll off the tongue easily. Fortunately, it wasn't *my name* that I intended for people to remember; it was God's.

Thanksgiving 2019 was one of the most enjoyable in decades. Having all 21 of our extended family members gathered around our dining room table is our tradition. But the Thanksgiving prayer that Ted wrote and shared before dinner was a reminder of how much his faith had grown throughout our cancer journey. He spoke boldly about the fact that we'd soon be celebrating Christ's birthday, and that this spring we'd celebrate His Resurrection, and that His death was payment for our sins. In closing, he shared that God is the source of all of our blessings.

After eating, we lingered at the table a while longer. We all seemed to take full stock of the present; we soaked in the presence of each one at the table, laughed at all the funny stories, and even broke into what had become our latest "thing," which was breaking into an extremely boisterous rendition of "Happy Birthday," at the top of our lungs.

(John, my 93-year old father-in-law, had long ago shared that when he was growing up in Greece he'd never had a birthday party. Not surprising then, he loved when we'd sing the birthday song to *anyone*, at *any time*, whether they had a birthday or not!)

While we were still at the dinner table answering questions we'd passed around the table per our tradition, my niece shared the news that she and her husband were expecting a baby, and as our "big fat Greek family" always did, they went *ballistic* with shrieks of excitement. This would be the first baby on both sides of our family.

Later, I found myself thinking about the first stages of a baby's life and yet also, the fact that I was feeling a bit older, not just because I'd recently turned 60, but feeling more of the emotional toll of the past few years.

At the very same time, I felt more alive than ever. I recognized God's prompting for me to narrow my focus for the upcoming year; to concentrate on writing and speaking to share my story of running a business, dealing with two cancers and the development of my faith — among other things. And the timing felt so right.

I thought back on the night in the hospital when God impressed upon me that we would be called to speak about the source of our healing for Ted. I was convinced that sharing the book I was writing (this book) would be the start of that assignment. I somehow sensed it would be deliciously frightening; I believed it was a privilege to do so, and yet also it would take a lot of courage and energy.

As He led me back to the passages of Luke, I saw for the first time that the one who'd come back to thank God for his healing, was a Samaritan, a foreigner — a misfit! Then as I reread the same passages, I saw that this man worshiped God in a *loud voice!* How ironic that I'd felt like a misfit and had been scolded and shamed for my loud voice! How many times had I been told, "Alicia, use your indoor voice." Or, when teaching aerobics classes I'd been told "You don't need a microphone because your voice is loud enough." *Again*, I saw how God can, and often does, use everything for good.

---

**And we know that in all things God works for the good of those who love him, who are called according to his purpose. (Romans 8:28)**

---

The day after Thanksgiving, we drove back to Rochester. Ted had another scan of his liver late that morning, and then early afternoon we met with Dr. Thor to hear the results. We were hopeful we'd hear good news, that the chemotherapy treatments he'd just completed had been successful. Unfortunately, that wasn't the case.

Dr. Thor shared that Ted's tumors hadn't shrunk and had actually grown a little bit. After talking through various options, he suggested taking a new approach to treating Ted's cancer. An interventional radiologist would perform several embolizations thereby cutting off the blood supply to the tumors in the liver. And without a blood supply tumors die.

That approach seemed promising and the potential side-effects would be tolerable so once again we got on board with the plan and started making all the arrangments; we cancelled work events, rescheduled personal appointments, changed our plans for our holiday gatherings, made hotel reservations and arrangements for dog care — and it all felt a little overwhelming. But as always, we tackled it one step at a time.

On December 1, I put up the Christmas tree. I joked that nothing put me out of the Christmas mood more than struggling to put up the lights and ornaments each year. I certainly loved the finished product, but I found the process laborious, and yet somehow I ended up being the one that tackled that chore.

It was an odd thing to be focused on the celebration and festivities of the Christmas season, and yet also be mindful of the unknown with Ted's cancer. Once again, I was learning to hold space in my head for two completely different thoughts and feelings, at the very same time.

---

**I was learning to hold space in my head for two completely different thoughts and feelings, at the very same time.**

---

I was finding that I had greater faith than I'd ever experienced before. Yet I'd occasionally been afraid. Sometimes I'd find myself thinking about the future and wondering if I'd be a widow. I wondered if Ted would be around to walk our daughter down the aisle if and when she got married. I wondered if he'd be by my side so we could grow old together. And I wanted that so badly.

Eventually, I'd return to the vision God had given to me; that He was going to heal Ted, but that it wasn't going to be a quick or easy "season." That made me excited, and I repeated one of my most common prayers, which was, "God, show off Your glory! Use every bit of our situation to draw others close to You." That always left me with a feeling of peace, and I looked forward to the coming year full of hope and thanksgiving. I reminded myself that we were in good hands, for we were in *His* hands.

On December 6 we were back in Rochester for the first embolization.

We'd previously had all Ted's other treatments at the Mayo Clinic, but this procedure would be done at St. Mary's Hospital. So that morning, prior to checking in, Ted, Kristin and I went to the chapel located inside the hospital. Unless my friend Diane had told us about it, we'd likely have missed it. I was so glad we didn't, because it was breathtakingly beautiful.

I'd imagined a small stark chapel, but this was huge, as big as many of the regular churches I've been in. Stained glass windows, marble everywhere, statues, and detailed crown molding — every detail was amazing.

The three of us (Ted, Kristin, and I) had the place to ourselves, which was very nice. Ted took a seat in one of the front pews, and Kristin and I stood behind him, placing our hands upon his back, and we prayed. We all shed a tear but had a great sense of peace as we left and found our way to get checked in for his procedure.

Unfortunately, they got behind in the procedure rooms, so we waited for two and a half hours before they even took us back to the prep room. Ted hadn't had anything to eat since dinner the evening before, and he was hungry and tired.

They finally wheeled him back for the embolization at 12:30 P.M. Dr. Andrews was the head interventional radiologist who did the procedure. Many of the staff told us that if they ever needed this procedure, they'd undoubtedly want Dr. Andrews to do it, which was reassuring to all of us.

The procedure was supposed to take between one and one and one half hours. But it only took 15 minutes! Afterward, Dr. Andrews said that Ted had great arteries, and that it went faster and smoother than they could have imagined. (I joked that him having great arteries was just one of the many reasons I married him!)

Instead of just going after a few specific arteries, Dr. Andrews embolized the largest arteries going to at least two-thirds of the right lobe of the liver. He shared that his plan would be to repeat the same procedure in January, and then again in February. He was hopeful that he could embolize all areas of the liver with just two more procedures, which was music to our ears.

He said regardless of the size of those that remain, he felt confident the embolization would be successful. At the same time, he warned us that the pain would likely be significant as Ted healed, given the size and location of the tumors that would now be dying.

My biggest prayer had been that God's presence would be evident to all that were involved with that step of the process. It was most definitely evident! The fact that they got so much accomplished in so little time and that Ted hadn't had the intense pain they'd predicted were signs that God had answered our prayers.

Unfortunately, upon being admitted and getting settled into a hospital room, Ted began to have pretty severe nausea. Due to the work going through the femoral artery, he had to remain on his back for four hours. It was horrible to see him throwing up while lying down. Each time, I tried to help him by supporting his neck and head, but it was awful to watch him suffer.

Later that night I went back to the hotel to sleep. Although I'd been hesitant to leave him I knew I needed sleep or I'd be no good to anyone.

• • • • • • • • • • •

## SCENE 18: SPIRITUAL GIFTS

The following week one of our pastors reached out and asked me to speak to a women's group about spiritual gifts. I was inclined to say, "no," but after praying about it I felt led to accept the invitation.

As I put together my presentation, I reflected upon the fact that throughout the past few years, many people's spiritual gifts had impacted me in significant ways. I thought of the woman who shared her prophetic vision with me about Ted being an old grandfather and living a long life.

I thought of my good friend, Kelly, and her gift of hospitality. She'd so often hosted me for a cup of tea or lunch, and a time of prayer. Given her exceptional knowledge of Scripture, her compassion and her heart for God, her prayers were beautiful; they'd been as uplifting and riviting as the melody of a beautiful song.

I thought of the woman at church, Lori, who blessed me with her spiritual gift of intercessory prayer (having the function of interceding prayer). Several times her prayers had been direct confirmation of what I'd sensed God had communicated to me. Consequently, the words she'd shared with me had been so comforting and encouraging.

I thought about the sermons I'd heard as I sat in church every Sunday morning the words God had provided through all of our exceptional pastors, and again, how often they'd aligned with what God had been guiding me to see or hear.

I was also mindful of the spiritual gifts that God had bestowed upon me. The gift of leadership that allowed me to continue to develop a coaching team for Wholehearted Living. Also, my spiritual gift of faith. Without a doubt, that gift had grown much deeper over the past few years and had been a substantial source of support — especially throughout our cancer battles.

In addition before I even knew what it was called — my gift of exhortation had been used through Wholehearted Living. The gift of exhortation includes encouraging Believers to mature in their faith, which I'd been doing through all of my teaching and coaching.

I also thought about how I'd been shamed throughout my childhood for my enthusiasm, my loud voice and my excessive talking. And I found it humorous that God has called me to enthusiastically encourage others by using my voice — in a book or from a stage. Who says God doesn't have a sense of humor?

I can't help but think about how many other people experience resistance to their own calling, because of their wounds. That thought is was energizes me to share the decluttering tools with every woman I possibly can.

I can easily envision the significant impact women can have on their families, their communities, and ultimately, the Kingdom of God if we learn to take our rightful spot in God's plan. That is what my heart longs for; for every woman (man and child, too) to live wholeheartedly! And, God willing, I'll use my last breath to enthusiastically encourage others to do just that: to love God, themselves, and others, with all their heart.

> "Jesus replied, 'You must love the LORD, YOUR God with all your heart, all your soul, and all your mind.' This is the first and greatest commandment. A second is equally important: 'Love your neighbor as yourself.'" (Matthew 22:37-39)

• • • • • • • • • • •

## SCENE 19: A NEW NORMAL

Over the next several weeks Ted continued to recover from the procedure. God's provision was evident because Ted continued to have no pain whatsoever, which was highly unusual. However, as a result of the embolization, his hemoglobin had dropped significantly. That contributed to his fatigue, shortness of breath, dizziness, and pale color.

With Christmas just days away, I felt unsure what to plan for our family celebrations. Due to Ted's limited energy, I didn't want to to schedule too many activities. At the same time, however, I desperately wanted to have some fun, to plan some outings with good friends and family, and to make it a wonderful Christmas for our adult children. It felt like a balancing act that I was ill-equipped to manage.

I felt incredibly blessed and realized things could certainly be much worse. Yet I'd learned the damage of minimizing feelings, so I acknowledged that I also felt a bit weary. I began to realize how different our "normal" routines had become, compared to three years ago before our cancers. Sometimes I'd felt connected and supported by so many people, and yet other times, I'd felt very much alone and disconnected. And those feelings had often changed throughout any given day.

Whenever I'd found myself moving toward worry, I'd reminded myself not to focus on how big our challenges were, but instead, to focus on how big God was. Ted's idea for the blog title of, "Faith vs. Fear" had been an important reminder to both of us. I knew prayer provided for the lack of pain after the first embolization, and I had no doubt God would ask us to trust Him equally for the next one.

In addition to Ted's current condition at that point, we'd also been dealing with other family health issues. My father-in-law had begun to fail and I'd found myself thinking Christmas might be the last holiday we'd have with him. That had made me sad but I also knew he'd said he was ready to be with Rose, his wife who'd passed away nine years prior.

John 16:33 makes it clear; in this world we *will* have troubles, but we can be at peace, knowing God has overcome them. This is not our true home, and when I'd reminded myself of that fact, I'd found my heart yearning for Heaven. No more pain or suffering and getting to hang out with Jesus — it all sounded pretty darn good to me.

Times like that prompted me to cry out to God, asking Him to send His Son to come again *soon* before even more suffering was endured by my loved ones. Yet, I also asked for mercy and for more time, since there were so many who didn't yet know their Creator and Savior.

One Sunday morning, I decided to go to church without Ted. He'd not slept well since we'd arrived home from the hospital and therefore he needed to go back to bed. Earlier that morning as I'd read my devotionals and talked things over with God, I'd anticipated that God would speak to me (at church) about something significant.

Once I'd arrived at church and settled into my seat, Jim and Janis Lovell came and sat beside me. (Jim is the cardiologist I've previously mentioned, and Janis is a friend and graduate of the Wholehearted Living program.) They asked about Ted and provided encouragement as I tearfully shared what we'd gone through over the past few weeks.

After the service was over, I felt an internal nudge to go forward to receive additional prayer. I spotted the same woman, Lori, who'd previously prayed for me. After greeting her, I shared that I felt like I was probably the *only person* who truly believed that God would heal Ted of cancer.

She closed her eyes and took a moment to listen for God's words. She then declared the words she was hearing from God; "Yes! Yes! Yes! Keep believing because I *am* providing a miracle and I am healing Ted!" At the same time I had an overwhelming sense of peace, and my heart soared.

She went on to say that she saw a huge green light, and that God was saying it was time for me to "go," and to use my gifts to share the messages

He'd given to me. Again, through the sharing of her spiritual gift, I received the encouragement and confirmation that I'd so badly needed. I left church that day with the strongest sense that it was time for me to share my story, and that 2020 was going to be a year of miracles.

---

**"With God all things are possible." (Matthew 19:26)**

---

• • • • • • • • • • •

# SCENE 20: MY YEAR-END REFLECTION

On December 24, as we prepared to celebrate Christmas Eve, I spent some time reflecting upon our past several years. Since January of 2017, the daily life we'd grown comfortable with had taken a detour we'd never seen coming.

Even the past few weeks had been unexpectedly tough. After getting home from the first embolization, Ted had struggled to have the energy to keep up with his normal schedule. He'd somehow managed to stay on top of work, but mostly while on the couch or in the recliner. He'd gone into the office for short periods of time, but just showering and getting there wore him out.

I'd been doing everything I could to help him and yet often felt helpless, as there was usually nothing I could do to make him feel better. At the same time, I knew the importance of self-care so that I could be my best for myself, for him and for others.

For my own sanity, I'd maintained my coaching business and continued to work on expanding the Wholehearted Living program. In addition, I remained committed to running again, for I knew how much it would help me emotionally, physically, and spiritually. It was often when I'd been running that I'd received major downloads from God, which I'd *loved*!

In talking with friends, I realized that many questioned whether we grasped the seriousness of Ted's diagnosis. We did. We knew full well that there wasn't any cure *(yet)* for neuroendocrine pancreatic cancer. Although it wasn't the more common, more deadly type, doctors made it clear that the goal was to buy time and learn to "dance with it."

Occasionally there were moments where I'd thought about the possibility that this could end Ted's life sooner rather than later. Yet at the same time, I had such a deep peace and hope that was unshakable.

Some people thought I was naively optimistic, but I knew that wasn't the case. Instead, my belief was grounded in God and what He'd told me. He'd provided visions for me, confirmation through scriptures, lyrics of songs, words of other people, dreams, and more. He'd given me every reason to believe He would heal Ted and that my job was to believe.

Sometimes it felt lonely, as if I was the one who believed that, and I was tempted to try and convince others what God had shown me. Fortunately, I'd realized that wasn't my job, and had left that in God's hands.

I'd continued to spend time praying throughout every day, thanking God for what I knew was a gift, for He'd used it to develop a greater faith than Ted or I could ever have imagined. It had also caused us to be more present in our daily lives and more intentional about our most important relationships. I more frequently told people how much they meant to me and I lingered a bit longer — especially when holding Ted's hand.

God continually brought me back to 1st Corinthians 2:9: "No eye has seen, no ear has heard, and no mind has imagined, what God has prepared for those who love Him." I knew God was still in the miracle business and was convinced we'd experience more of His miracles in the coming year.

---

**"No eye has seen, no ear has heard, and no mind has imagined, what God has prepared for those who love Him." (1st Corinthians 2:9:)**

---

At that point, we knew Ted would likely have another embolization prodedure and we were hopeful he'd soon be in remission. The next step would be to find an oral chemo or something to keep him in remission. Even better, in my mind, was the anticipation of when God would provide complete healing.

The next morning we'd celebrate our Savior's birth, and because I knew He was alive and well, I was confident the best was yet to come! (Jeremiah 29:11)

---

**". . . Everything is possible for one who believes."
(Mark 9:23)**

---

●●●●●●●●●●●

# CLOSING SCENE: COMING FULL CIRCLE

It feels rather unsettling to wrap up a story without an ending to share. But I believe that's the point; this book is about how to live when we *don't know* what the future holds, especially in the midst of life's biggest challenges.

Although it might sound alarming, it's a fact that we're all facing death — none of us are getting out of here alive. It's just that most of us don't know what will be the cause of our death. Somehow, with a stage four cancer diagnosis, it can make one's death feel much more imminent. Yet that may or may not be the case. Heck, any one of us could get hit by a bus tomorrow!

Regardless of the number of days we'll live on this earth, we can make the best of every one of them. We can (and must) put our faith into action, and the keys to do so are: Declutter your life, claim your true identity, and embrace your purpose *with passion.*

God has made it clear that He's given me a purpose, and a passion, and that I'm to do the following: I'm to share my story *and* the decluttering process that helped me to develop a vibrant and healthy relationship with myself *and with Him.* So ready or not, imperfections and all, I'm **taking the stage!**

# INTERMISSION

*Time for a stretch, a potty break,*

*and a chance to grab something to eat.*

• • • • • • • • • • •

## WARMING UP THE ORCHESTRA FOR
## THE THIRD AND FOURTH ACTS

Now that you have heard my story and have been introduced to some of the tools for living wholeheartedly, it is your turn.

Are you tired of feeling stuck, disconnected, lonely and overwhelmed? Are you sick of being busy and feeling unfulfilled? Are you ready to experience change in your own life? If so, it is no accident that you are still reading.

As you already know, God downloaded these simple tools that helped me to declutter my life and my relationships. However, make no mistake about it; I'm not finished, for this is an ongoing process and will last a lifetime. At the same time I've learned to live with a tremendous amount of peace, an inner confidence and great joy — despite cancer, running a business, experiencing loss and a variety of other challenges.

It is time for me to share the steps to declutter, so you can get started with the process. My prayer is you will take those steps with some help from others, and in doing so, will learn to live *wholeheartedly* — being who you are created to *be* and doing what you are created to *do*. Ultimately, you will find that nothing could be easier or more rewarding.

# ACT 3

## *Your Relationship with Yourself*

· · · · · · · · · · ·

## SCENE 1: THE PAIN AND PROBLEMS OF AN UNHEALTHY RELATIONSHIP WITH YOURSELF

Our relationship with ourselves is what causes most of our pain, anguish and frustration in life. That is good and bad news. The good news is that you don't have to wait on anyone else to change so you can experience a healthier relationship with yourself. The bad news is that you have no one else to blame.

---

**The relationship with ourselves is what causes most of our pain, anguish and frustration in life.**

---

Although we often point to others as the source of our frustration or failures, it usually comes back to our own issues. Maybe you have heard the expression that if you point a finger at someone else, four fingers are pointing back at the real problem, which is you. God's Word says it this way:

---

**"Why do you look at the spec of sawdust in your brother's eye and pay no attention to the plank in your own eye?" (Matthew 7:3)**

---

### YOUR DRUG OF CHOICE?

Like most women, I used to have a toxic, unhealthy relationship with myself. Although at the time, I had no idea that relationship was in such bad shape. I was not even remotely aware of the baggage I was hauling around with me. I thought — no, I *believed* that I was not good enough — not smart enough, pretty enough, successful enough, but also, too much. So what do you do with all of that? You numb out. You choose a type of drug to try and alleviate the pain.

Some women choose drugs or alcohol. Others choose to numb out with food, or excessive shopping, or overworking, or exercising. I on the other hand chose people pleasing and performing. Although those were more socially acceptable drugs, they were very damaging.

However, it looked good — at least from the *outside*. But on the *inside* I was exhausted and lonely. I was tired of feeling like I was trying fight my way around unseen obstacles. I kept trying new approaches but never reaching whatever achievement I had been working toward. Unfortunately, my own perceived failures and shortcomings fueled my addictions.

Other addictions are more prevalent in the news but do you what drug is most socially accepted today? It is not opioids or any of the other common drugs you might think of. The most socially accepted drug of today is the addiction to being busy.

At the risk of sounding like The Church Lady, (Dana Carvey's character on Saturday Night Live), do you know that BUSY is an acronym? It stands for, Being Under Satan's Yoke. Keeping us busy is one of the enemy's greatest spiritual weapons. If he can keep us busy and distracted we'll fail to make our biggest impact. We will fail to focus on what matters most, *doing* what we are created *do*.

**IDENTITY THEFT**

In today's world we often hear about the need to protect ourselves from identity theft. Sadly, however, we fail to realize we have been victims of it; we have been robbed of our true identity and therefore, we're living with a false one. When you were under-aged a fake ID may have allowed you entrance into a bar, but today, trying to be someone you're not is exhausting and can leave you feeling alone, misunderstood and unlovable.

Who is currently in charge of your identity; who is controlling your thoughts about yourself? Is your mother, father (or someone else from your past) still directing those thoughts? Or, are you now an emotionally healthy adult, able to take responsibility for your own thoughts?

Who do *you* think you are? Do you think you are capable or incapable; intelligent or stupid; successful or unsuccessful; likeable or unlikable; strong or weak? Let's face it, you believe a lot of things about yourself. Have you ever considered that at least some of those things might not be true? Chances are that you are not who you think you are, hardly anyone is.

---

**Chances are that you are not who you think you are, hardly anyone is.**

---

## HEAVY BAGGAGE

Unfortunately, previous generations were not inclined to get help from a therapist or counselor. As a result, they usually ignored their own wounds and unhealthy patterns. In many homes parents taught their kids to sweep things under the rug rather than equip them with coping skills to handle some of the challenges of everyday life.

Since we all carry unfinished business from previous generations and then we accumulate some of our own, it shouldn't come as a surprise that we encounter trouble. Jesus said that in this world we *will* have troubles, and *boy* was He ever right! Eventually, hopefully, we will come to the realization that our heavy baggage is weighing us down and causing a lot of problems.

## FATHERS

In the book *Captivating*, authors John and Stasi Eldredge share that girls are in essence born with some weighty questions deep inside. Those questions are: Am I beautiful? Am I worthy of being pursued and cherished? Am I important enough for your time and attention? To gain an answer to those questions, girls look *first* to their fathers.

Good fathers answer those questions (through their words and actions) in a positive way. Consequently, their little girls are free to fully discover who they are, which is critical to becoming who they were created to be. They learn they are loved and valued and as a result are more apt to become confident, secure women.

If on the other hand they have an unhealthy relationship with their father, where there's insufficient protection, provision and interaction, girls may struggle to find the truth of who they are. They will often find it hard to connect with their father and consequently, to connect with themselves — at least with their most *authentic* self.

For many women the relationship with their father wasn't what they had expected or hoped for. What about you? What was your relationship with your father like in your childhood, when you were developing your core beliefs about yourself? Might it be contributing to your pain? Could it be related to the way you treat yourself?

## MOTHERS

It is commonly assumed that little girls are to be nurtured by their mothers. Isaiah 66:13 (a) states, "As a mother comforts her child, so I will comfort you." In this scripture, the Lord was referring to His comforting Israel like a mother comforts her child. This is just one example of the standard or expectation of every mother to comfort her own child.

In the relationship with her mother, a little girl will experience her first and most powerful taste of either acceptance or rejection. Depending on the health of that relationship, or lack thereof, she'll get completely different results. When a little girl is accepted by her mother she'll often develop confidence and happiness.

If on the other hand the little girl is rejected, she'll likely be left with insecurity, frustration and even shame. When mothers are preoccupied or for some other reason emotionally available, their daughters often end up with a never-ending supply of critical thoughts about themselves. Sadly, that's all too common.

## BEING A CRITIC

One of the problems that causes resistance to having a healthy relationship with ourselves is that we've learned to become our biggest critic. We treat ourselves worse than we'd treat any of our enemies. That is unfortunate, for we cause most of our own pain and anguish — pain and anguish that is otherwise *completely* unnecessary.

I often ask audience members to jot down ten things they do not like about themselves. Nearly all of them start writing without any hesitation. Then, I change the directions — asking them instead, to write down 10 things they LIKE about themselves. You would be amazed at the change in pace; most struggle to come up with even two or three items.

Because I've been coaching women for going on 20 years, I'm not at all surprised by their responses. Plus, most of us don't have to be told that we are our own toughest critic; we are well aware of it.

A critic is defined as a person who expresses an unfavorable opinion of something. It comes from the Greek *kritikos*, which means judge or decide. Another word for a critic is enemy. An enemy is defined as someone actively opposed or hostile to someone or something. Are you actively opposed or hostile to *yourself*?

How you treat yourself directly affects how you treat others. If you are extremely critical of yourself, chances are good that you are also critical of others in your life. If you are constantly critical of yourself, it will be challenging to offer kindness and encouragement to others. The good news, however, is that as you learn to give grace and forgiveness to yourself, you'll naturally extend the same to others.

---

**How you treat yourself directly affects how you treat others.**

---

## WE CARRY GUILT AND SHAME

Who among us has not done or said some things we've later regretted? To some degree or another we have *all* made mistakes — and that is just a byproduct of being human. However the most damaging consequences of our mistakes can come from holding onto guilt or shame.

As a reminder: Guilt is feeling bad about something *you have done,* whereas shame is feeling bad about *who you are.* Shame goes deeper and can have a more devastating impact.

Guilt and shame are heavy bags that we were not intended to carry. Jesus paid the ultimate price for us to be free of guilt and shame. If we are determined to hold onto those, we're in essence telling Him that what He did was not enough — it was not enough for *our* mistakes. Certainly that must break His heart.

Carrying around guilt and shame is anything but helpful for your relationships — whether the relationship you have with yourself, with God or with other people.

As mentioned before, in the process of decluttering my past I learned to treat myself as I would a good friend; in place of judgment and condemnation, I extended forgiveness, grace and mercy to myself. As a result, I no longer carried guilt and shame, which was exactly as God desired.

---

**Carrying around guilt and shame is anything but helpful for your relationships — whether the relationship you have with yourself, with God or with other people.**

---

## SCARED OF THE BEAST

Because we have been so hard on ourselves for so long, we have reinforced a negative opinion of ourselves. We have added to our ever-growing list of perceived shortcomings. Therefore we are scared to connect with this beast we think we have become; we want to avoid ourselves like the plague and we imagine keeping that beast stowed away in the depths of our imaginary basement.

What is ironic, is when we get help and go to uncover that beast we've tried to hide, we usually find it was nothing more than a stuffed animal; it was harmless other than the stories we have been telling ourselves about it. You can hardly imagine the relief clients feel when they realize that for themselves. Often, they say it feels like getting out of jail. They just hadn't realized the keys to their freedom had been in their own hands.

## PRIDE

On the other side of the coin, maybe we have spent years working really hard, trying to make it appear that we have it all together. To admit we are not as perfect as we might look can be tough, but it can also bring relief — after dealing with the underlying issue, which is pride.

Pride is defined as having an excessively high opinion of oneself. If pride is on one end of the spectrum, feeling worthless is at the other end — and neither one is healthy. Developing a healthy relationship with yourself, God and others, involves a balance; being humble *and* having the confidence that stems from valuing who you are and relying on God.

## FEAR OF FEELINGS

Another problem that causes resistance to a healthy relationship with ourselves, is our fear of feelings. Have you ever stopped to think about why we are so afraid of *feeling* our feelings?

Our fear of feelings is based upon stories of the past, from our childhood. It is our interpretations of the feelings that are distorted and keep us stuck, not the feelings themselves. It is the stories we have repeatedly told ourselves about the feelings that make them feel so scary. Avoiding our feelings is a problem, because it keeps us operating as children; instead, facing our feelings allows us to function as adults.

When expressing our feelings we often send mixed messages to ourselves and to others. For example, you will hear people say things like "I feel so frustrated. I hate that I can't lose weight and get healthy. Yet, I know many people have a lot more to lose than I do, so I should be happy with who I am." Which is it? If you hate something, it sounds like it matters a fair amount to you. Or, does it really not matter? See how easily we can mishandle our own thoughts and feelings?

Failure to respond appropriately to feelings can be hurtful and cause damage in any of our relationships. Most people do not share their feelings with you so you can fix them. Most often they simply need a safe place to share what is on their mind, to share what they are feeling and thinking. Usually they know what to do and even how to do it. However, until they can share their feelings and thoughts and feel they've been heard, they cannot seem to move forward and take action that would be beneficial.

When we continually suppress our feelings we cause major havoc on our body's ability to function properly, which in turn decreases our immune system and opens the door to illness and disease. In a sense we can make ourselves sick by suppressing our feelings.

---

**Routinely suppressing our feelings is damaging to our bodies — emotionally and physically.**

---

Eventually, feelings that are buried will cause unhealthy, dysfunctional behaviors such as: compulsive eating, perfectionism, people pleasing, anorexia and others. It is all too common to try to stuff our feelings by stuffing our bodies with food. I cover that subject in much greater detail in my book, Your Relationship with Cravings, but the reality is that no substance can ever satisfy the emotional hunger you may have stuffed deep inside. Usually the issue is not with food; it is with yourself!

Our bodies are designed to express and process feelings much like the way we digest and eliminate food. Unfortunately, many people have been stuffing their feelings so long that it is as if they have a chronic case of emotional constipation. That is not healthy! However emotional *incontinence* is equally unhealthy. As you learn to regularly process your feelings you will be much less likely to experience either end of the feelings spectrum that can be messy and downright harmful.

## FALSE PEACE

A healthy homelife is safe and loving. It is like a peaceful meadow that allows you the freedom to run and play — also to share your thoughts, feelings, questions, concerns. It allows you to dream, to grow *and to thrive!*

Unfortunately, rather than a peaceful meadow, many little girls grew up in the equivalent of an active land mine. Were you by chance one of those girls?

One day you stepped to the right and all was well. The next day you took the same step only that time there'd been an explosion. Your young mind struggled to try and make sense of it all, but you couldn't. Eventually you felt paralyzed and were afraid to move.

If you grew up in an environment like that you probably learned to become invisible; you became good at withholding your thoughts and feelings and abandoning your wants and needs. Sadly, the combination of all of that stunted your growth.

Often those types of homes are the training ground for girls who become adult women that settle for false peace. They learn to say whatever is necessary so they do not cause any waves; they do not want to risk upsetting the temporary stillness and are afraid that one wrong move could prompt more outbursts or even abuse.

Sadly they can pay a hefty price for keeping false peace. They can feel unnoticed, unimportance and unqualified. In turn, that can lead to significant stress and things like passive/aggressive behavior, feeling isolated, discouraged and lonely.

## BE NICE

Another factor that contributes to an unhealthy relationship with ourselves, is that as women, we have been trained to be nice. We're told to keep quiet, let others go first, and be lady-like.

For far too many women this has resulted in a hesitancy to speak up, to step forward and share what we have; we undervalue ourselves and what we have to offer, and *that is* a big problem! We have failed to make the connection between being nice and being confident, as if being both is not an option. But it is!

## BLIND SPOTS

We all have blind spots but those we do not acknowledge will continue to blind us. In other words, without getting help we will struggle to identity the things that are keeping us stuck and preventing us from the results we want — with our friends, families and other relationships.

On the other hand, if we get help to deal with our blind spots, we can avoid a lot of the damage we would otherwise cause. We can learn how to process unfinished business from our past so we can embrace our present and be hopeful about our future. Keep in mind that it would be a rare person who could identify and process their emotional and spiritual clutter on their own. The truth is we need each other, and often a trained professional.

## DISTANCE FROM GOD

One of the worst pains that we can experience is the pain of feeling distant from God. And make no mistake about it; if there is distance between ourselves and God, *we* are the ones responsible for that distance. Not God.

Interestingly enough, most of us think we are to make everything about God. However, when we do not like ourselves (the women whom He created) our actions are more likely about ourselves. We may take meals to the sick, teach Sunday school and participate in a Bible study — which are all great things, but our actions stem from the belief that we are not good enough. So under the surface, it is really all about us!

In contrast, if we make it about ourselves to the degree that's necessary to declutter our lives, we'll be free to surrender to God's agenda and our actions can be about Him. Do you see the difference? In other words, we must first make it about ourselves so we can then make it all about God. Hence the importance of investing in yourself, to develop and maintain a healthy relationship with yourself, before trying to draw close to God. It does not mean we are to exclude God and become self-centered. However, it does mean making yourself and your wounds a priority, so you can truly give yourself to God for His use.

## IN REVIEW, THESE ARE THE PROBLEMS THAT CAN CAUSE PAIN IN OUR RELATIONSHIP WITH OURSELVES:

- We have been robbed; we are living with a mistaken identity
- We carry baggage from our relationship with our father and/or mother
- We have become our harshest critic and biggest enemy
- We have not processed our mistakes and therefore, carry guilt and shame
- We are scared to connect with the beast we think we've become
- We have become prideful, rather than humble
- We are afraid of our feelings and often send mixed messages

- We have learned to settle for false peace — which is stressful and anything but peaceful
- We have misunderstood what it means to be nice, so we withhold our valuable contribution
- We are unaware of our blind spots and the damage they're causing
- We do not like ourselves and therefore feel distant from God

• • • • • • • • • • • •

# SCENE 2: HOW TO DEVELOP A HEALTHY RELATIONSHIP WITH YOURSELF

Developing and maintaining a healthy relationship with yourself is the way to experience greater peace, confidence and joy. It is also a huge part of learning to live *wholeheartedly*.

## DECLUTTER

To *develop* a healthy, vibrant relationship with yourself, decluttering is required. Decluttering means to get rid of or greatly reduce the clutter in our lives. In other words, to get rid of the *stuff* that weighs us down and causes resistance to living wholeheartedly.

The Bible addresses decluttering in different words but the core message is the same; Hebrews 12:2 states, "Let us strip off every weight that slows us down."

---

**"Let us strip off every weight that slows us down."**
**(Hebrews 12:2)**

---

Decluttering your relationship is similar to cleaning out your clothes closet. You first open the doors to the closet and take an inventory of what you have. Next you determine what you want to keep, what needs to be mended, sold, given away or thrown out. Then, you follow through to get things where they belong.

In regard to developing a healthy relationship with yourself, the steps would be much the same: Take an inventory of that relationship; identify what you want to keep, what you want to change and what you want to get rid of. Then follow through with action steps that are helpful.

When broaching the subject of decluttering, most people automatically think of physical clutter. However, there are two other types of clutter; *emotional* and *spiritual* clutter are equally, (if not more) important to deal with. In fact, physical clutter is often the result of emotional or spiritual clutter.

## SLOW DOWN TO GAIN FOCUS

Sadly, a busy life has become the norm rather than the exception. Women are trying to juggle far too many things and often resemble a hamster running on a hamster wheel; frantically trying to move forward, but getting nowhere. Have you every stopped to think about what drives you to run at such a frantic pace?

If you love and value something, you take good care of it. So what do you believe about yourself that allows you to run yourself ragged, trying to cram more and more activities into your daily schedule?

---

**Why do you make a habit of overscheduling and demanding so much of yourself? And how do you justify such harsh treatment of yourself?**

---

## AWARENESS

An important step in improving the relationship you have with yourself, is to become fully aware — 100 percent present and conscious. Unfortunately, many people are still encumbered by unfinished business from their past or worried and stressed about the future. Both prevent them from living in the present. Becoming fully present, aware of everything you are thinking, feeling and doing, is a vital step towards living wholeheartedly.

## ARE YOU WILLING TO CHANGE YOUR THINKING?

Having a healthy relationship with yourself requires having an open mind and being willing to change your thinking. Romans 12:2 tells us not to be conformed to the patterns of this world, but rather, to be *transformed* by the renewing of our minds.

We have all been conformed to the patterns of our own families and friends, and we have been influenced by a variety of sources — including the media. The question is, are you willing to re-examine what you have been led to believe? Are you willing to learn the God-given truth and tune out all the other voices in your head?

---

**The question is, are you willing to re-examine what you have been led to to believe and to align it with God's truth?**

---

## THE FAMILY SOUP

As you sort through your past you may find yourself wanting to choose a side; you might think that you can either honor your parents or you can address your wounds and unmet needs — those of that little girl within you. You'll need to choose both!

Each one of us must extend grace and forgiveness to our parents. And *at the same time* we must provide compassion and kindness to ourselves; we must validate our hurts, hungers and unmet needs.

Doing both is the key to getting free from your past without dishonoring or bashing your parents. It's a win/win scenario because everyone gets what they need. The following analogy can help you to see the wisdom in this approach:

Imagine that your parents' job was to provide a hearty soup to give you what you needed to grow and thrive. However, their own parents were only able to provide them with a thin, tasteless broth. So that is what your parents started out with.

Your parents may have been more fortunate than most and were eventually able to plant a vegetable garden in their back yard. Consequently, they were able to add some chopped vegetables into the family soup, but not until you were *much* older. The broth you grew up with was nothing special; it was the equivalent of providing adequate shelter and a place for you to sleep.

Sadly, they never managed to purchase any cows or chicken, so they did not provide any meat. Nor did they acquire any seasonings. Therefore, it's not a surprise the soup they provided lacked some important things.

Without any meat you failed to get some important nutrients that were essential for developing into the adult you were created to be. For example, a safe and loving place in which to discover who you are, make mistakes and learn from them with parents who treated you with patience, kindness, grace, mercy and love.

As if that was not bad enough, without vegetables and seasoning, you missed out on other key ingredients — things like modeling and teaching you how to take responsibility for your honest thoughts and feelings, how to speak up with your wants and needs and how to deal with conflict.

Given that scenario, would it make sense to get angry and yell at your parents, shaming them for what they didn't provide? Of course not. They could'nt give what they did'nt have.

At the same time, however, that doesn't change the fact that you didn't get some of what you needed. We *all* have God-given needs; emotional, physical and spiritual. And when those needs are not met they can and often do stunt our growth and development — our *emotional and spiritual* growth and development.

## IT TAKES COURAGE

To develop a healthy relationship with yourself, you will need to discover who you really are, and that will involve stepping out of your comfort zone into uncharted territory. You may be apprehensive at first, but remember that the perfect guide dwells within you; you are filled with the Holy Spirit who is truth itself. You have been perfectly created with a purpose and passion and many in the kingdom are waiting for you to walk into your destiny and into their lives. That will not happen if you stay where you are, stuck in your comfort zone.

Most women will have to leave behind the belief that who they are is not good enough or defective in some way. They'll have to let go of the harsh, critical relationship with themselves which has become all too familiar. Cheri Huber, author of, Seventeen Lies That Hold You Back, says it like this: "It takes a tremendous act of courage to admit to yourself that you are not defective in any way whatsoever." So how courageous are you? Are you courageous enough to discover the truth of who you are; are you strong enough to discover and celebrate the incredible woman that God created in you?

---

**It takes a tremendous act of courage to admit to yourself that you are not defective in any way whatsoever.**

---

## IT TAKES TIME

The relationship with yourself is not a one-time event; nor is it something to occasionally tend to. This is about an *ongoing* relationship. As with any relationship, it will take some time. It will not happen overnight but, starting today, you can begin to make changes and improvements to that relationship.

## A FAN

What does it mean to be a fan? Do you have a sports team that you follow of which you would consider yourself a fan?

What about yourself? Do you consider yourself a fan of you? What does a fan fan do? Typically they cheer for them and spend time and money supporting them.

To develop a healthy relationship with yourself you'll need to become your own fan. You must learn to cheer for yourself and to encourage and offer support to yourself. That'll include spending time, money and energy on yourself.

To be a fan you must first connect with the heart of that little girl or younger woman who resides in you. In other words, to connect with the real, raw you! That will involve identifying her wounds from the past and determining what caused them. Then it will be important to listen to what she thought and how she felt. Most important of all, is to uncover what she believed about herself *because* of what she went through. That is crucial to identify before moving on.

## LET GO OF CONDEMNATION

As you go back and examine your life up to the present there are two roads you can choose. While the road of acceptance and includes grace, mercy and forgiveness; the other is the road of rejection which includes judgment, unforgiveness and shame. While the road of acceptance leads to life, the road of rejection leads to condemnation, and death. Romans 8:1 says, "There is no condemnation for those in Christ Jesus." So why would you continue to reject yourself and be so hurtful?

When you learn to let go of condemnation your life will transform. It is amazing how much life you can experience when you are no longer repeatedly beating yourself over the head with an imaginary 2 x 4.

---

**When you learn to let go of condemnation
your life will transform.**

---

## OFFER GRACE

When connecting with yourself as a little girl (or younger woman) it will not be enough to just to let go of condemnation, nor will that be easy. You must fully connect with her hurt and humiliation and then provide understanding, compassion and forgiveness to her. You'll need to take over the nurturing of your heart, specifically in regard to those most hurtful memories.

## KEEP YOUR PROMISES

Each time you have failed to do what you have said you will do, you have unknowingly caused damage to your relationship with yourself. How many times have you failed to eat healthy, go to the gym or say no to others, even though you previously said you would do so? Like most of us, you probably have a long record of being untrustworthy. Therefore, it will take time to rebuild that trust.

From now on, when you make a promise to yourself, it will be vitally important that you keep that promise. Every time you do so, you'll build strength and integrity within that relationship. Also, when you are working to build trust, it's crucial that you *under*-promise and *over*-deliver, and not the other way around!

With each choice you make to honor and support yourself, you will prove your heart can be safe with you. As a result the real you will be able to come out of hiding, be fully present and vibrantly alive.

## PRACTICE

When you think about it, it takes effort for *anything* to become effortless. Anything that is now easy for you, at one point in time was probably uncomfortable and difficult. Consider a hobby, for example knitting. When I first held a pair of knitting needles in my hands it felt strange; I found it awkward to hold them while at the same time placing the yarn where it needed to be.

With practice however, I became more comfortable with the process. Eventually, with enough repetition I mastered the art of knitting. Now it is something I can do without even thinking about it.

The same principle applies with getting wholehearted and developing a strong, healthy relationship with yourself. Practice and it will get *much* easier!

## GET HELP

We all have areas that, for whatever reason, we can not see clearly; in other words we fail to see things as they really are — things that can often cause catastrophic damage. Therefore, we are wise to get help to identify and remove what's obstructing our view.

## TAKE RESPONSIBILITY FOR OUR THOUGHTS

A thought repeated often enough can become a deep-seated belief. And our beliefs can dig ruts. Unfortunately, it takes a lot of work to get out of a rut.

When taking responsibility for our for our beliefs three steps are involved: Identify the belief; question the belief; and then make a choice. You can choose to discard the belief, replant the belief, or plant an altered version of the belief. When questioning your beliefs, ask yourself the following:

1. Could the belief include some errors?
2. Does holding onto the belief serve a purpose?
3. Does the belief streamline or scatter my energy?
4. What has the belief cost me in the past?
5. Currently, what is the belief costing me?
6. What will the belief cost me in the future if I continue to hold onto it?

For example, do you still believe you cannot cross the street without holding someone's hand? That is probably something you believed at some point in your past but not anymore. What about your belief in Santa Claus; your belief that you'll never be successful; the belief that you're not good enough, smart enough or attractive enough?

## HANDLE FEELINGS EFFECTIVELY

If you are serious about becoming a fan, you must learn to identify, express and process your feelings. Feelings are defined as an emotional state or reaction. Feelings are not right or wrong, they are simply how you feel.

Feelings are not to be fixed. Feelings are simply *for feeling*. However, feelings can only be fully expressed in a safe, welcoming environment. If people fear they'll be criticized or rejected for their feelings they'll be resistant to share them.

One way to illustrate what needs to happen to feelings is to think about going to a fast-food restaurant. Imagine that you pulled up and placed your order. Then the employee restated your order to ensure that it was correct; that it was what you wanted to receive. That is exactly how we should handle feelings.

When people share their feelings with you, the best response is to reiterate what you heard. That will allow you to verify the accuracy or inaccuracy of what you think you heard. All too often, what we *think* we heard is not what was actually said. Then we run off with false assumptions that bring frustration and other problems.

Imagine back at the drive-thru you ordered a chocolate shake. Then the employee said, "You don't really want that. Wouldn't you rather have a salad, because a salad is much healthier for you?" Can you imagine how you would feel? Outraged or at least very frustrated? Sadly, we do something similar with others and their feelings. We try to convince them they should not feel what they are feeling; and instead tell them what they should be feeling. My motto is: Never *should* on yourself — or anyone else!

Once a feeling is expressed, validation is the only thing that it necessary to free the owner to move on. If feelings remain without validation it is like putting a cork in a bottle of soda that was shaken up. The feelings will build up energy and eventually explode. When that happens it's not going to be good for anyone involved!

## IDENTIFY YOUR FEELINGS

At first when you try to connect with your feelings it may feel a little awkward. Do it anyway. And practice, again and again and again.

If you're not connected with yourself at a heart level, you may struggle to identify what you're feeling, thinking, wanting and needing. So the first step may simply be to stop and quiet yourself. Then ask yourself out loud, "What am I feeling right now?" Take a breath and listen. You might also consider keeping a running list or a journal of all your feelings.

## EXPRESS YOUR FEELINGS

After you have identified your feelings, the next step is to express them. When you were an infant or small child expressing your feelings came easily and naturally. When you were hurt, you cried. When you were mad, you put a scowl on your face, hit something or said something to express that. Over time you learned that sometimes it was not okay for you to share how you honestly felt. Sometimes that would bring hurt to others, or bring discipline on yourself or a variety of other undesirable outcomes.

As a result, you learned to stuff, deny or avoid some of your authentic feelings. Doing so is what started to harm the relationship you have with yourself. It was just one more way that you were beginning to conform to the patterns of this world, and in particular, to your own family system.

Could it be time for you to renew your mind; to establish the truth about your own feelings? Do you need to learn that it is not only okay, but sometimes completely necessary, to get mad and express your anger? Do you need permission to grieve a loss from your past? Could it be time to discover your own voice and speak up for what you think, feel, want and need?

Maybe it is time to learn how to identify and express your feelings honestly. Give yourself permission to feel what you feel and to express those feelings; to do so is crucial to a healthy relationship with yourself, with God and with others.

---

**Maybe it's time to begin identifying and expressing your honest feelings, even if at first it's a little awkward.**

---

## VALIDATE FEELINGS

What does it mean to validate feelings? Simply put, validating feelings is giving people the message that their feelings are legitimate. Validating feelings means giving people (yourself and others) permission to *feel* the *feelings*. Sometimes the most powerful response you can give a person — whether you agree with them or not, is to simply say, "You have every reason to feel that way."

To illustrate responses that are very common but *not* at all helpful, consider the following situation. Your good friend has shared with you that she just lost her job. If you replied, "At least you have your health and your fmaily," that would be an example of dismissing feelings.

An example of spiritualizing the feelings would be to say: "Well it's a good thing you know God is in control and He'll take care of everything." If you responded with: "All you need to do is get to work on updating your resume," that would be an example of telling people what to do and thereby disregarding their feelings.

Again, those types of responses are *not* helpful and can actually be hurtful. All anyone needs in response to sharing their feelings is to receive validation; to get the message that they have every right to feel what they are feeling. Giving someone that message does *not* mean that you necessarily agree with their feelings, but that you are simply acknowledging what they're feeling.

---

**All anyone needs in response to sharing their feelings is to have them validated; to be given space in which to feel what they are feeling.**

---

When you reach a point where you can face and process even feelings that are uncomfortable, you will quit trying to numb out or self-medicate with food, exercise, work, shopping or anything else. Addressing your feelings opens the door to your heart, but addictive behaviors essentially close the door and lock it.

## DISCOVER YOUR LIKES

In 1999, Julia Roberts starred in the movie Runaway Bride. There is a significant scene in the movie where Julia's character is asked by her current fiance what type of eggs she likes. Sadly she is unable to answer because she does not know.

With each of her previous fiancés (there had been several) her character had always chosen to like whatever *they* liked; she'd developed a bad habit of going along with whatever they'd wanted and therefore, abandoning her own wants and needs.

In a subsequent scene she prepares eggs in every way possible; she makes scrambled eggs, poached eggs, fried eggs and eggs benedict. For the very first time she tries to discover what *she* likes. She tries to determine what it is that she really wants and needs.

How well do you know what you want and need? How effectively do you communicate your wants and needs to those who are in a position to help with them? If you don't know what you need, it will be unlikely that your needs will be met. Taking care of your relationship with yourself involves taking good care of your needs.

## TENDING TO YOUR NEEDS

To declutter your relationship with yourself, you will need to identify your needs. You will want to look at how your needs have been treated in your past as well as the present. While growing up, were most of your needs met or neglected? What about now?

Also, because our needs change as we go through different stages of life, it is important to reassess our needs on a somewhat regular basis. How long has it been since you've taken an inventory of your needs?

If you are aware of your current needs, do you make them a priority? Many women have denied their needs for so long that to focus on them is really uncomfortable. Therefore, a crucial step to developing a healthy relationship with yourself is to come to the realization that self-care is not selfish. In fact self-care must become a priority!

Although it is not illegal, when we avoid self-care we end up paying a hefty fine! However, please do not misunderstand my point. I am not suggesting that we are to *only* be concerned with ourselves, but that *is* where it starts. We are not often capable of giving to others what we have not first given to ourselves. That includes forgiveness, grace, compassion, mercy and kindness. Living wholeheartedly involves extending each of the above to yourself, and then to others.

---

**Although it is not illegal, when we avoid
self-care we end up paying a hefty fine!**

---

## GUARD YOUR HEART

To be a fan of yourself you will need to excel at being a guard. What do guards *do*? Ideally, they keep bad things out and welcome good things in. Right? What is the current status of your role as a guard? Are you doing a good job protecting the woman who resides in you, or do you deserve to be fired? God's Word makes it very clear: "Guard your heart for it is the wellspring of life." (Proverbs 4:23) Guarding our hearts is not just the icing on top of the cake, it is one of the main ingredients!

---

**God's Word makes it very clear:
"Guard your heart for it is the wellspring of life."
(Proverbs 4:23)**

---

## LOOK AT GOD'S WORD

Lastly, but most importantly, what does God's Word say about having a healthy relationship with ourselves? Matthew 22:39 says to love your neighbor as yourself. The assumption is that you do, in fact, love and *like* yourself. Sadly, most of us have been kind, compassionate friends to our neighbors, yet we have been extremely harsh critics of ourselves.

If you struggle to treat yourself kindly, maybe you are still operating with a false identity like we've previously talked about. If you believe you are a disappointment or a burden, you are sadly mistaken. Instead, you must learn to live with the truth — that God loves you and delights in you.

What about your value? How valuable do you think you are? How valuable does God say you are? In the parable of the lost sheep we learn that even if 99 of His sheep were with Him and you were the one who had strayed, He would drop everything and come to find you. Sounds like you are pretty valuable to Him.

Luke 12:24 says that you are more valuable than those who He clothes and feeds every day. Matthew 10:30 says you are so important to God that He has numbered the hairs on your head. Obviously His words show that you are incredibly valuable to Him. What about God's actions? God sent His only Son to die just for you. Can He show you any clearer how valuable you are?

God wants nothing but the very best for us in all things. He is our biggest fan and He is not okay with us bashing ourselves or treating ourselves poorly. He loves us, always. He repeatedly forgives us and extends grace to us. Can you say the same?

The truth is that everybody is somebody to God. Each one of us is unique, invaluable and irreplaceable in the heart of God.

God created everything good in Heaven and earth. Yet when He looked at it all, He decided the world was not complete without YOU. You are irreplaceable in the heart of God.

**LET'S REVIEW THE STEPS TO DEVELOP A HEALTHY RELATIONSHIP WITH YOURSELF:**

- Declutter your past; sort through your memories, wounds and unmet needs
- Slow down, become aware and learn to be fully present
- Keep an open mind, realizing that some of your beliefs are at least partially untrue
- Be courageous and willing to leave your comfort zone
- Become your own fan (rather than your worst enemy)
  - Connect with honest thoughts and feelings, your hurts, humiliations and wounds
  - Let go of condemnation
  - Offer grace, forgiveness and encouragement to yourself; treat yourself like a best friend or a neighbor
  - Keep your promises; build integrity and trust
  - Practice being a fan and get outside help to be successful at it
  - Take responsibility for your thoughts
  - Handle feelings effectively; validate your feelings — and those of others too
  - Discover your LIKES and tend to your needs
  - Guard your heart
- Look to God's Word for guidance and claim your true identity

• • • • • • • • • • • •

# SCENE 3: THE BENEFITS OF A HEALTHY RELATIONSHIP WITH YOURSELF

There are tremendous benefits from decluttering your relationship with yourself and learning to love *and LIKE* who you really are.

As you learn to develop and maintain a healthy relationship with yourself, you'll get more comfortable treating yourself with the same patience, kindness and compassion that you so easily offer your best friends. You will learn to value and enjoy your own unique personality, talents and experiences. As you do, you will find yourself moving out of survival mode and into growth and fulfillment.

A healthy relationship with yourself can provide a newfound confidence. Consequently, you will be free to try new things, discover new interests, and welcome new possibilities. In addition, when a woman is confident she carries herself differently, she makes an entrance differently and she speaks differently.

When you learn to value who you are, you will no longer hold yourself to ridiculous, unattainable standards. You will lose the need to prove anything to anybody — most especially to yourself! Consequently, you'll be able to kiss those perfectionistic standards good-bye.

One of my own examples can help you to see several of those benefits:

One day a friend of mine invited me to join her and another friend for an early morning bike ride. I am usually quick to jump in and participate if something sounds fun, so I did.

Bright and early the following morning, I loaded my bike into the car and began driving out to where we were going to meet. On my way I began thinking about some of the things I had failed to ask — details that would have been important to know *before* agreeing to the bike ride.

There are two different scenarios that could have played out. First, had I still been my own critic my self-talk would have sounded something like this:

*"Geez! I can't believe how stupid I am! Why didn't I get the details?! Sometimes I have the attention span of a gnat! I should have found out how long they plan on riding, what distance they will cover and what time we will likely finish. I have probably gotten in over my head and once again, that was a stupid thing to do!"*

Can you relate to some of the negative comments I could have hurled at myself? Had you been in the same situation might you have said something similar to yourself?

That is the way I used to treat myself. However, although it is an ongoing process, I have come a long way; I have learned to treat myself like a good friend and therefore, my reaction was quite different. I put my hand over my heart and said out loud:

*"Oh Alicia, you are delightful. I love your enthusiasm and willingness to jump in and have fun; I love that you are always up for a new adventure and meeting new people. It is okay that you did not get all the details, as connecting with people and getting some exercise is what you were focused on. And guess what? The great news is that we (me and my heart) can ride for as long as we are comfortable and then we can turn around and come back home. I will be happy to speak up about the right decision for us and to encourage them to continue on without us.*

Notice *none* of the *situation* had changed; what changed was my self-talk — and there was a huge difference between the two conversations I could have had with myself. One would have left me feeling emotionally beat-up, embarrassed and ashamed. The one I chose was encouarging and made me feel valued, supported and celebrated.

That one example might seem insignificant, but imagine making that type of self-talk (and self-care) a *lifestyle*. Doing so can change your life *significantly!*

## FREE OF COMPARISONS

How great would it feel to no longer have the need for comparison? Does it sound too good to be true? In today's world of Facebook, Instagram and other social media options, it can be so easy to compare your *imperfect* life to the occasional seemingly perfect photos of others.

As clients have decluttered their relationships with themselves, they have enjoyed their ability to see others' posts - without being envious or having the need for comparisons.

## EMOTIONAL TEFLON

As a child, most of us had a strong desire to fit in rather than stand out. Therefore, we tried to be as similar as possible to everybody else. In addition, we were strongly influenced by others' opinions.

As an adult, when you have a healthy relationship with yourself, you'll no longer fall prey to negative comments from others. Confident in your own opinions, other's comments will no longer stick. It will be like having a coating of emotional Teflon!

I strongly believe that someone else's opinion of you does not have to become your opinion. Eleanor Roosevelt said it this way: No one can make you feel inferior without your consent.

---

**As you develop a healthy relationship with yourself, others' opinions of you will be much less important — and after all, what others think of you is none of your business.**

---

## ENCOURAGING OTHERS

When you LIKE who you are you will more easily provide affirmations and encouragement to yourself — and you will find those overflowing to others. Then, instead of needing to put others down, you will be able to help build them up. And doing so will feel fabulous!

When you have developed a healthy relationship with yourself you will find the confidence to speak the truth in love; you will be equipped to speak up honestly. No longer being an imposter, you'll enjoy the satisfaction of being your most authentic self *and* being a source of encouragement for others.

## NO LONGER ADDICTED TO BEING BUSY

Another great benefit of a healthy relationship with yourself, is that you will lose the addiction to being busy. No longer running at a frenzied pace like a hamster on a wheel, you will be able to slow down and be more intentional about how you invest your time, energy and money. You will also be able to rest, without feeling guilty.

Also, from being well-rested, you will have greater focus. You will no longer allow your energy to be scattered by distractions and trying to multi-task. As a result, you will find it less stressful and easier to reach your goals.

Yet another benefit of maintaining a healthy relationship with yourself, is that you will no longer be stuck in your past, or worried about your future. Consequently, you'll find it easier to be fully present, making the most out of every day.

## INCREASED ENERGY

When you learn to maintain a healthy relationship with yourself, you will likely find an increase in energy. You will be surprised at how much better you feel when you are no longer beating yourself up most of the day, *every* day.

## HANDLING MISTAKES

How do you handle mistakes? If they are your own mistakes, are you defensive? Do you point the finger at others and try to avoid taking responsibility for them?

In the process of liking yourself you will learn to extend grace more easily. When grace flows freely you can accept your mistakes, as well as those made by others.

Realizing that *everyone* makes mistakes you can view them as opportunities to learn and grow. Then you'll no longer waste time beating yourself up for them. Instead, you can take responsibility for your actions and then move on without carrying even an ounce of guilt or shame.

Closely related, is the freedom to ask questions without the fear of judgment. When you learn to be confident in who you are and are no longer berating yourself for your perceived short-comings, you will become more comfortable with being curious. That includes getting comfortable asking questions, trying new things and asking for help.

Another benefit from a healthy relationship with yourself is that you will be better equipped to receive constructive criticism. Realizing everyone has blind spots, you can more easily allow others to help you see what you can't see on your own.

Yet another benefit, is that you will no longer take things personally that aren't personal. When you're a supportive fan of yourself, you'll be less offended by others. Consequently, you will experience much less drama, and that is a benefit *everyone* will enjoy!

Another benefit is that you will be free to use your pain to help others; sharing your previous painful experiences (when appropriate) can help you value your pain. It may also help you recognize how God can use it for good, by having you connect with and encourage others by sharing those experiences with them.

## USING YOUR TALENTS

When your relationship with yourself is thriving you will no longer shrink back and withhold what you have to contribute. Instead you will be free to use your talents, gifts and experiences exactly as God desires. You will find fulfillment in using them to help others, while also helping yourself.

## FOUNDATION FOR A RELATIONSHIP WITH GOD

Lastly, the greatest benefit of developing and maintaining a healthy relationship with yourself, is it provides the foundation for building a vibrant relationship with God. He loves you and, until you're able to love the one He created in you, it'll be hard to experience His love.

## REMINDERS OF THE BENEFITS OF DEVELOPING AND MAINTAINING A HEALTHY RELATIONSHIP WITH YOURSELF:

- The peace that comes from treating yourself kindly
- Enjoying the freedom and confidence to try new things
- Relief from letting go of perfectionistic standards — for yourself and others
- Increased energy from positive self-talk
- The joy of being free of the need for comparisons
- The stability of wearing emotional Teflon (and dealing with less drama)
- The joy of more easily encouraging and affirming others
- The peace from no longer being addicted to a busy life
- Increased energy to do what matters most to us
- The ability to handle mistakes with grace (and no longer carrying shame)

- Being well-rested and having better focus
- Using our talents for our own benefit and those of others
- Having the solid foundation for developing a vibrant relationship with God

# ACT 4

## *Your Relationship with God*

• • • • • • • • • • •

## SCENE 1: THE PAIN AND PROBLEM OF AN UNHEALTHY RELATIONSHIP WITH GOD

Have you ever felt that God is distant? Have you wondered why He seems so far away or so uninvolved? If you are like most people, chances are good that you have at least *occasionally* had thoughts like these.

The truth is God has given Himself to you completely. He is not holding out on you or anyone else. He is always 100 percent with you and for you. Therefore, if there seems to be distance, we are the ones responsible for putting it there.

Imagine that life is a riverbed. God is at the head and we are down river from Him. We are designed to continuously receive Him, the "living water;" we are created to be dependent on the Lord, the only true source of water.

So what happened? Unfortunately we were wounded along the path and, consequently, we learned to believe some things that are simply not true. We have distorted thinking about ourselves, others and even about God. And collectively, all of that junk caused resistance to the truth.

In the riverbed of life our wounds gathered mud and moss along the way. Over time they developed into large boulders that caused resistance to the living water. Hence we became parched and assumed God must not have been interested, or He was distracted or ignoring us. Thankfully, nothing could be further from the truth.

It is not uncommon to find ourselves operating as if we are independent lone rangers, when in fact we are created to be completely dependent on

God. If we are not connected to God through a personal relationship with Him, we will quickly lose our way. We can find ourselves in scary places that feel like our worst nightmare, being places God never intended for us to be.

Maybe you are someone who is not yet aware of God's love for you and His desire to have a deeply personal and vibrant relationship with you. If that is the case, you will likely continue to search for something — that *one thing* that you believe will bring the satisfaction, peace and joy that you crave.

That searching can cause you a lot of pain because, no matter how long you chase a carrot on the end of the stick, it will fail to bring you what you had hoped it would. That can lead to feeling discouraged, depressed and disillusioned. That search can also cause you to waste decades of time and inordinate amounts of energy and money — all costs that could have been avoided.

## OUR RELATIONSHIP WITH OUR FATHER

I have previously addressed the influence of a girl's relationship with her father and some of the collateral damage one may have from that relationship. However, in addition to it greatly affecting her beliefs about *herself*, it's often a prelude to her relationship with God. A girl's relationship with her father is usually her first significant and lasting interaction with a male authority. Consequently, her beliefs about her father can generate many of her beliefs about other men — especially God.

Based on your father's words and actions, did you come to believe God was loving or unloving, patient or impatient, reliable or unreliable? Did your father routinely keep his word to you, or did he more often break his promises to you? How did those experiences affect your expectations of God?

Was your father your greatest protector and advocate, or a harmful critic? Did your father model how to treat a woman; did he treat your mother with love and respect? And, did he treat you accordingly? Did he provide the message that you could do anything you sent your mind to, or, that you would never amount to anything?

Unfortunately many women never consider the impact of their

relationships that have contributed toward their beliefs about God; they overlook wounds that cause significant pain — or at the very minimum resistance in their relationship with God.

## RELATIONSHIP WITH OURSELVES

Part of the problem that can cause resistance to a great relationship with God is, not surprisingly, our relationship with ourselves. Yep. If you are still emotionally beating yourself up, then you will have a hard time experiencing God's love.

That is because although you desperately want to be loved, you've come to believe that you're unlovable. Since your desire and your belief are diabolically opposed, you will inevitably block God's love. How sad since the thing you want most is literally so close.

## MISSING PUZZLE PIECE

Imagine working on a one-thousand-piece puzzle. Your neck and back pain are indications of being slumped over a table for hours as you have labored to put it together. You cannot imagine the amount of time you've spent searching for the right piece for just the right spot. Then when you get down to the last few pieces you realize you are missing one. You do not have the one puzzle piece needed to complete it! You look around on the floor, under the table, under the puzzle box and are frustrated that you have put all this effort into something that is not going to bring the satisfaction you'd hoped for.

That is similar to the feeling of trying to live life apart from God. He is the biggest and most important piece of the puzzle of life. If you get distracted and pursue all the other pieces at the expense of having the most important single piece, you'll fail miserably. You'll miss out on living the best life possible; the one God created for you. Obviously living a life without God is much more catastrophic than failing to complete a puzzle, but you get the idea.

## REVIEW: THE PAIN AND PROBLEMS OF AN UNHEALTHY OR STALE RELATIONSHIP WITH GOD

- We feel distant from God, which leads to loneliness and confusion,

getting lost and experiencing trouble
- We operate as independent lone rangers, rather than as dependent children of a Father with unlimited love, wisdom, capabilities and resources
- We waste time, energy and money, that could all be avoided
- We miss out on God's best blessings, including not fully experiencing His love
- We continue to search for something and look in all the wrong places, not realizing that HE is the only thing that can fill that hole in our hearts — similar to missing the most important piece of the puzzle.

• • • • • • • • • • • •

# SCENE 2: HOW TO DEVELOP A HEALTHY RELATIONSHIP WITH GOD

Every day you are either growing closer to God or more distant from Him. There is no in between. Does that thought make you squirm? Hopefully not. But how would you describe your current relationship with God; as vibrant and fresh or dull and stale?

Developing a more meaningful relationship with God involves making some disciplined choices. You must intentionally choose to make Him a priority. That involves capitalizing on opportunities to connect with Him and get to know Him.

A meaningful relationship with God includes making a choice to accept Jesus as your Lord and Savior. Some people are very willing to choose Him as their Savior, as if that's like having fire insurance. However one must also choose Him as their Lord. That means giving up their life, their plans and their timing — for His! Have you done that? If not, there's no better time than the present.

## STUDY GOD'S WORD

Although there are many options available to most of us, one of the best ways to develop a great relationship with God is to dig into His Word. Bible apps and other online resources can be super helpful but there is simply no replacement for holding the Bible in your hands and reading God's Words.

As you flip through the pages of the Bible, do not be afraid to underline passages you find meaningful. At a later point when you look back through scriptures you previously underlined, you will probably find that they have a different and fresh impact. It can feel like certain words were specifically meant for *you* at that very moment. That is a great way to experience God geting your attention and speaking to you.

---

**As you flip through the pages of the Bible, do not be afraid to underline passages that are meaningful to you.**

---

If you are intimidated to dig into the Bible, get some help to do so. Remember that in the earliest stages of my own faith I purchased a children's Bible. It was easy to understand and helped me become familiar with the most common Bible stories.

As our faith grew, my husband and I joined a couples' Bible Study group. We met every other Wednesday night and would work our way through a particular book of the Bible or just discuss the previous sermon from church. Our faith grew substantially because of our thorough discussions and we learned a lot from sharing our questions and hearing others' insights, as well as sharing our own.

If you are serious about studying the Bible, you might be interested in a method that I was introduced to early in my faith journey. It's called the SOAP method and is an acronym which stands for: Scripture; Observation; Application; and Prayer.

"S" prompts you to record the scripture you read. As you write out the words in each verse, you will increase your familiarity with the words of God, His disciples and others who documented the inspired words from God.

"O" indicates observations you make within the scripture. Record things you notice, like the people involved, the location or the main issue being addressed.

"A" reminds you to look for ways to apply the scripture. Ask yourself, "How does this pertain to my current life?" Consider how you might put these words into action.

"P" prompts you to pray. Record a prayer to God. Include any praise, questions or requests you might have in response to the scripture you just read.

This SOAP method is just one of many options, but can provide a systematic approach to reading and studying the Bible. Whatever method you choose, if you stick with it you will not only increase your knowledge of God, but you will also experience a deeper connection with Him.

As Paul instructs us in Colossians 3:16, the words of Christ should live in our hearts and make us wise. As we marinate in God's Word, we see that it can be life changing. Hebrews 4:12 says, "For the word of God is full of living power." Aren't you anxious to connect with that power?

---

**We must study the words of God so they become familiar and begin to impact our daily lives; among other things they should become a source of wisdom, clarity and comfort.**

---

## DECLUTTER

Like any of our other relationships, our relationship with God has some clutter that could use some attention. So how do we get rid of the junk that clutters our relationship with God? As you now know, to declutter anything (whether your closet or your relationships) the same three-step process is required: First, take an inventory; second, make a decision about what to do with each item; and third, take action steps.

In addressing your relationship with God you must first take an inventory of your beliefs and your behaviors. What exactly *do you* believe about God? How do you think He feels about you? What do you believe are His hopes and plans for you? What about your behaviors? How are you approaching and interacting with God? Are you doing things that are helping or hindering your relationship with Him?

The next step is to make decisions; determine your beliefs that do not line up with God's words and, therefore, need to be discarded. Also, identify behaviors or actions that are not contributing to the relationship you want to have with God.

The third step then, is to take action. Get rid of what is no longer serving you well. Stop the damaging behaviors and begin to establish new ones. Replace the faulty thinking — about God and your relationship with Him, with truthful statements that align with His words.

There are several other things that can also help you improve your relationship with God: rest; repent; and relinquish.

## REST

What do you think of when you hear the word rest? Is it taking a nap, lying on the beach somewhere or sitting on the couch with your feet up? Although rest *might* include these things it often just means to be still.

Psalm 46:10 says, "Be still and know that I am God." If you never slow down long enough to be still, how will you know that God is speaking to you?

Remember that BUSY is an acronym for: being under Satan's yoke. If you think you are busy, maybe it's time to identify what you are missing because of all that busyness. It might be preventing you from the very thing you are designed to need and want most — a close, personal relationship with Jesus.

God is not impressed with all that we take on. He does not approve of our living life at such a frantic pace, cramming more and more into our already busy schedules. Instead He wants us to learn to rest.

For those of you who are parents, you may especially relate to the following experience of mine: I used to attack every day with tremendous energy, determination and a *long* to do list. I routinely overscheduled myself and tackled more than was feasible for anyone. One day, however, God gave me a picture that stopped me right in my tracks.

He brought to my mind how my children (when they were little) would routinely take naps. I would then peek into their room to check on them. Even in the event of a very challenging morning, when they were at rest it melted my heart. It brought me joy to see them so peaceful. As I was remembering how that made me feel, He said to me, "I feel the same way when you are at rest." From that moment on, I approached resting with a whole different paradigm.

---

**The Sabbath was a crucial part of God's creation for He knew the benefits of resting.**

---

## REPENTANCE

What do you think of when you hear the word repent? Is the image that comes to mind that of an angry person wagging his or her finger at you? Hopefully not. The Hebrew word for repent is *shuv*. It means to turn around or to turn from; turn *from* your sin and turn *back* to God. It implies a change — a change of direction, a change of heart or a change in behavior.

Sadly, many people have received discipline that was sometimes less than loving. Consequently, they have a warped understanding of repentance. Is that the case for you? Did you usually feel shame and guilt after getting disciplined? If that was your experience, I am so sorry. That was never God's plan.

Unlike some of your childhood experiences, everything done in God's house is done with love. He disciplines us out of love. He asks us to turn away from what He knows will bring us harm and turn back toward Him. He knows that through our obedience we experience the greatest blessings He has prepared for us. Repentance brings an opportunity to remove anything that is between us and God. It is therefore a privilege, rather than a burden. We don't *have* to repent, we *want* to.

## RELINQUISH CONTROL

Matthew 16:25 states, "For whoever wants to save their life will lose it, but whoever loses their life for me will find it." Whose life is it? Are you still asking God to help you live your life, or have you learned to let Him live His life from within you? If we're desperately holding on to our own life, we won't be able to reach for His. If we are going to receive life on God's terms, we must relinquish life on our terms. The great news is that what He has in store for us is much better than anything we could come up with on our own.

Matthew 16:25 states, "For whoever wants to save their life will lose it, but whoever loses their life for me will find it."

We have heard it before, but we are the clay and God is the potter. When you come to understand that our plans pale in comparison to those of God's, it becomes much easier to let go of our own. It is like our grandest hope is to become an ashtray when God intends to shape us into a breath-taking vase — one that carries flowers and other beautiful arrangements.

## COMMUNICATE WITH GOD

Healthy relationships require good communication. That seems fairly obvious, but good communication involves speaking *and* listening. In other words, healthy relationships involve dialogues rather than monologues.

Developing a healthy and vibrant relationship with God requires talking with Him *and* listening.

In Psalm 139:17 David writes to the Lord, "How precious to me are your thoughts, God!" In verse 23 he goes on to say, "Search me and know my thoughts." Apparently, David realized the importance of both *speaking* and *listening* to God. We are wise to do the same.

## TALK WITH GOD

How often do you talk with God? Does even the thought of doing so make you uncomfortable? Or, is it something you do regularly and are therefore quite comfortable with?

Did you grow up with parents who modeled having a relationship with Christ? Were they part of a church community that helped you develop a meaningful faith and an appetite for God's Word? Or, were you spiritually malnourished?

The great news is that regardless of your parent's preparation or lack thereof, it is never too late to establish and develop a vibrant relationship with God. It is like wanting an Oak tree; the best time to plant an Oak tree was decades ago, but the second best time to plant it is *today*. And when you think about it, the only thing we will take with us when we leave this earth is our relationship with our Creator, Father God. Hence it is a pretty important relationship to focus on.

## GOD LISTENS

---

### Jeremiah 29:12 states, "Then you will call on me and come and pray to me, and I will listen to you."

---

When you speak to God you can be confident that He is listening. Jeremiah 29:12 states, "Then you will call on me and come and pray to me, and I will listen to you." There it is! God's word clearly states that He will listen to you. What do you think after reading that statement? Do you believe God listens to you occasionally, but has more important things to be concerned with? Do you think He's perturbed when you pray and ask for small things? Do you believe God listens to you, but He's disappointed and frustrated with your requests or prayers? Or, do you believe God actually enjoys listening to you?

---

### What's the source of your beliefs? Where did you learn about *how* and *when* God communicates with you?

---

## ASK

Scripture tells us that we don't have because we don't ask. It is a simple question, but have you *asked* God to speak to you? If you are serious about developing an intimate, ongoing personal relationship with Him, why not start asking Him to communicate clearly and effectively with you? (James 4:2, Matthew 7:7-8)

## GOD SPEAKS

Scripture teaches us that God spoke in a variety of ways: He spoke through fire, trumpets and a still, small voice; He spoke through prophets and miraculous signs; He spoke through sermons, through storms — and the list goes on and on. The point is He spoke, and He *still speaks*. He continually looks for opportunities to speak to you and interact with you. The questions is, do *you* look for opportunities to listen and hear from *Him*?

## LEARN TO LISTEN TO GOD

Do you regularly practice listening to God or is it something you have only dreamed of? Do you think God is holding out on you and remaining silent? In John 10:27 Jesus said, "My sheep recognize my voice; I know them, and they follow me." Obviously then, He is speaking to us or we would never recognize His voice.

---

**In John 10:27 Jesus said, "My sheep recognize my voice; I know them, and they follow me."**

---

I used to say, I'd really like to hear from God but He is going to have to send me an email. It was pretty sad, but that is what I believed at the time. Eventually, as He led me to the concept of living wholeheartedly, He began to show me that He was, in fact, speaking to me; not just once in a while, but on a regular basis. It was not in the form of an email, but it was just as direct.

When I began to try and connect with God, I still believed that He was too busy to bother with me. In addition, I feared that if He did talk with me, I would hear the countless ways He was disappointed in me. (Obviously debris from my relationship with my own father that needed to be decluttered.)

It was quite a process, but over time I learned that nothing could be further from the truth. I came to understand that God is always ready and waiting to communicate with me, and with you. I had no idea that I would eventually experience God delighting in spending time with me — and what a relief that turned out to be!

## DREAMS

Some people hear from God most often in their dreams. In Matthew 1:20 it says that an angel of the Lord appeared to Joseph in a dream and spoke to him. Have you ever received a message from God through a dream or vision?

Fairly often, while I'm praying before going to sleep, I ask God to speak to me through my dreams. Since I'm considered a "talker," I kid around and say that I think God speaks to me most when I'm sleeping, for that's when He's more likely to get a word in!

I ask that while I'm asleep God will allow me to interact with Him, and to gain clarity about what to do to be obedient to His will. As a result, I often wake up with a vivid picture or dream that provides the direction I have prayed for. If you have not tried this approach to hear from God, why not give it a try? What do you have to lose?

## CONFIRMATION

One of the best ways to confirm what you are hearing from God is to record it — literally, word for word. Get a pen, paper and then quiet yourself. Pray and ask God what He wants to say to you; let God write a letter *to you*.

Start God's letter to you with an appropriate salutation. For example, Dear Little (your name) or Dear One, or something else that comes to mind. Then, just allow the pen to hit the paper.

Many clients assume this is quite presumptuous and certainly makes them anxious. That is simply an indication of their beliefs about God that need some attention.

As addressed before, imagine going to God as your loving, protective and compassionate Father and sharing what's on your mind. After doing so, you ask Him to talk with you and offer His advice. It would be unthinkable for Him to remain quiet or make it difficult for you to hear what He has to say. Instead, He is thrilled when you come to Him and share what's on your mind — and He is equally happy to share His thoughts with you.

It is perfectly natural to question whether the thoughts you write are in fact those of *God* or whether they are your own. Disregard those doubts and continue writing. After all, God is bigger than our own thoughts and can speak to us regardless of any resistance we may have.

Let Him share whatever comes, and then when you feel the letter is finished, pause. Ask Him if there is anything else He wants to share with you. If not close the letter with an appropriate signature like, Love, Your Father in Heaven, or All my Love from your Father who delights in you, or something else you feel led to use.

When you are finished, consider asking God for confirmation through other sources. Then close in a prayer of praise and thanksgiving. Be on the lookout over the next few days, for ways that God will confirm His message to you. You might even go back and reread the words from the letter that you previously recorded. More often than not, you will see key words or phrases that are not common for you to use; you realize they are not *your* words.

Another way to check for confirmation of what you heard is to determine if it is in line with God's character and His written word. God's voice and guidance will *never* go against His nature or His Word.

---

**God's voice and guidance will *never*
go against His nature or His Word.**

---

## TAKE A LEAP OF FAITH

To experience God's best we must not only release our perceived control, we must be willing to take action. That'll require venturing into unfamiliar territory. Doing so on our own would be nearly impossible, so to take that leap we must have faith in God; hence the phrase, a leap of faith.

Looking at Biblical history, we can relate to the problem the Israelites faced. They had a dilemma: they could follow Moses out of Egypt, or they could remain slaves in their homeland. In the hopes of experiencing Canaan, the Promised Land, they had to leave what was familiar and pursue a new life. Though they grumbled and complained throughout their exodus, God continued to guide them. With a cloud by day and a pillar of fire by night, God led them toward the Promised Land.

Today we find ourselves with the same dilemma. We can choose to leave our land — the life with which we have become so comfortable, or we can stay right where we are and miss out on what God has prepared for us. It would certainly be tragic to cling to our comfort zones instead of experiencing the incredible adventures God has prepared for us.

Do not panic. This does not mean that we are all called to pack our bags and head to a far off country. Rather, consider the times in your life where you realize that what you have been holding onto must be let go. In those instances fear can quickly rise to the surface. Fear reflects our inability to trust the one who invites us to take that leap; it shows our lack of faith.

---

**Fear reflects our inability to trust the one who invites us to take that leap; it shows our lack of faith.**

---

The more you get to know God, the easier it is to take that leap of faith. As we put our faith in Him, we become empowered to leap. As we contemplate our dilemma, He asks us, "Do you know how much I love you? Do you understand that what I have for you is much better than what you're holding on to? Do you trust that I'll guide and protect you?" So in return, what is your response?

Once we take that leap of faith we discover God's best. As we wholeheartedly say yes to Him, we experience His unbelievable provision. Then we no longer cling to our old comfort zones. Instead, we cling to God and find the greatest comfort in being with Him.

---

**Living wholeheartedly involves no longer clinging to our comfort zones and instead, clinging to God.**

---

## SPIRITUAL GIFTS

As you study the Bible you will discover that God has a marvelous plan for each one of us. And as part of that plan God has given us spiritual gifts. The purpose for these gifts is to help build the body of Christ and therefore, even though we are the recipients of them, they are intended for the benefit of others. They include: Faith, wisdom, serving, teaching, encouraging, giving, leadership, mercy, and exhortation — just to name a few.

If you do not yet know your spiritual gifts, there are a variety of assessments that you can take online at no charge. It would be wise to complete one or more so you can find out what yours are. Read the descriptions that are provided and then use that information to find the right opportunities to put your specific gifts into action.

## SPIRITUAL DISCIPLINES

Though spiritual gifts are given to us, when it comes to spiritual *disciplines* we are provided with a choice; we get to choose which ones we will use. Whereas spiritual gifts can benefit others, spiritual disciplines are primarily for *our own* benefit.

Spiritual disciplines are access points or methods for connecting with God. They include: Prayer, fasting, solitude, fellowship, worship and more.

To utilize spiritual disciplines, we must use some discipline or self-control. What comes to mind when you hear the word discipline? Do you think of harsh or shaming punishment? Hopefully not! Discipline is actually intended to be a *good* thing; it is designed to lead us to blessings like health and happiness.

God's word says that He disciplines those He loves. Don't we do the same? How loving would it be, for example, to raise a child without any form of discipline? Even your relationship with food, money and possessions must involve some discipline. The truth is that all healthy relationships involve some discipline.

We can so easily get distracted and discipline can help us stay on track. Discipline is also used to correct disobedience. As we participate in spiritual disciplines, our focus is drawn to God's presence and power in our lives; it promotes obedience which leads us to greater intimacy in our relationship with Him. James 4:8 tells us to draw close to God so that he will draw close to us. Again, what a privilege!

---

**Practicing spiritual disciplines allows us to connect with and draw closer to God. James 4:8 tells us to draw close to God so that He will draw close to us.**

---

Today, given our overly scheduled lives, silence may be one the most challenging discipline to practice. Psalm 46:10 says, "Be still and know that I am God." If we are running through life at a breakneck speed it will be difficult, if not impossible, to recognize and respond to God's presence in our lives.

For spiritual disciplines to be effective, they must be practiced on a consistent basis. This does not mean you aim for perfection and lose sight of the motivation for practicing them, but instead, that you make a concerted effort to do so on a regular basis. The motivation must be love and a desire to encounter God. Although they require some discipline, they are never meant to be a burden or a drudgery.

Think about how you most effectively connect with God. Is it through prayer or when you sing or perform worship songs? Could it be time that you sit quietly in His presence or time spent in nature admiring His creation? Or, maybe it is through reading and studying His Word or participating in Biblical feasts.

There are countless options available and one is not better than another. However, if you are serious about having a healthy relationship with God, you need to find ways that are meaningful and effective *for you*. Spiritual disciplines are meant to enhance and support your growing faith and your relationship with God.

---

**The motivation for practicing spiritual disciplines must be love and a desire to encounter God; they are to enhance and support your growing relationship with Him.**

---

## WORSHIP

The Christian life is not meant to be a solo endeavor. Instead it requires community. An important step to having a strong and growing relationship with God (living wholeheartedly and having a strong faith), is to gather together and worship as a community. It is hard to describe the difference that regular worship with a group of fellow Believers can make in your faith. Listening to the music, the sermons and getting involved in helping — it can all add depth to your faith and the quality of your relationship with God.

## RECEIVE AND GIVE

Your spiritual growth is not just for your own benefit. Instead, it equips you to teach and encourage others in their faith journey. It is a Biblical principle to receive and then share with others. It is as if we are in a jungle and are struggling to find our way through all the trees. As we come upon the next obstacle someone who has gone before us can reach a hand back and help us; they can show us the way to move forward. In return, we are then positioned to extend a helping hand to someone who is now in the position in which we had previously been.

Memorizing verses of scripture can also be helpful for yourself and for others. You would be surprised at how God's Written Words will surface when talking with others, and what a source of wisdom or encouragement they can be.

In addition, the more you learn to anticipate God's presence and power in your life the more you'll recognize both. It is similar to buying a new bright orange car and then feeling like everywhere you look you see others in an orange car. Your status or condition changed, and in the process, it opened your eyes and your awareness was heightened. The same can happen in your recognition of God's provision for yourself and for others.

In His infinite wisdom and love for each one of us, God often shows us just enough to take the next step. He knows all too well that if He showed us too much of our future we'd likely panic — because we would not yet be prepared for it.

However, He stands ready and willing to take us by the hand and lead us one step at a time. By the time we arrive at that future spot, we will be equipped to handle it. In technical terms that's called progressive revelation. All that means is that God reveals His perfect plans for us, in manageable bite-sized pieces. Another reason for doing so, is that at times we might be tempted to skip off on our merry way and forget our dependence upon Him. Either way the results would be disastrous, and He loves us too much to allow that to happen.

## LEARN AND GIVE

God is all-knowing and we are not. However, we cannot let that be an excuse for getting comfortable and satisfied with our current level of knowledge. If we let that happen we will miss out on experiencing a lot of what God has prepared for us. Whether you've never opened a Bible or you have a master's degree in seminary, there is always more to learn to develop a great (or *greater*) relationship with God.

Giving yourself permission to continue to learn and seeking opportunities to grow will undoubtedly help your relationship with God. Yet that is not enough. We must also be a source of knowledge and encouragement to others. The kind deeds we do for others means a lot to God; His Word says it is as if we have done those kind deeds specifically *for Him*. (Matthew 25:40)

Being a parent I can relate to this because when people do nice things for my daughter or son I am always grateful. Apparently God feels the same way. In addition, He knows that we are blessed when we give to others — and they are too. (Acts 20:35)

## LET'S REVIEW THE STEPS TO DEVELOP A VIBRANT AND FULFILLING RELATIONSHIP WITH GOD

- Establish a relationship with God by choosing Jesus as your Lord and Savior
- Make disciplined choices to connect with God and make Him a priority
- Study God's Word
- Declutter your relationship with God; sort through your beliefs about Him
- Rest
- Repent; turn away from your mistakes and turn towards Him; to do so is a privilege
- Relinquish control of your life; receive His life in exchange for yours
- Identify and use your spiritual gifts to benefit the body of Christ
- Practice spiritual disciplines to connect with God
- Communicate with God
  - Talk with God
  - Ask God to speak to you

- Listen to God; document His letter to you
- Confirm what you heard from God
- Take a leap of faith
- Keep learning and sharing what you learn with others
- Do nice things for others knowing that pleases God's heart

• • • • • • • • • • •

# SCENE 3: THE BENEFITS OF A HEALTHY RELATIONSHIP WITH GOD

## ASSURANCE

We might live to be a ripe old age but regardless, our years on earth are microscopic when compared to eternity. So the greatest benefit of having a personal, vibrant relationship with God is living with the assurance of spending eternity with Him in Heaven. And eternity is a *long* time!

But what about now? Hebrews 13:14 tells us that regardless of our address this is not our permanent home. When you understand that the here and now is only temporary your perspective will dramatically change; you will no longer sweat the small stuff, and that paves the way for less conflict and stress. Even better, is our ability to live with a confident hope, one that is firmly established in the knowledge that God is an overcomer and the best is yet to come. (Jeremiah 29:11)

## LOVE

The second greatest benefit of maintaining a personal and vibrant relationship with God, is to experience the love of your Creator, Father God — right here and now! We are wired for love and as you experience God's love you will find it more satisfying than anything else.

In addition, as a result of experiencing God's love, we can become willing vessels through whom God can share His love with others. Another benefit is that we more easily stay in line with His steps and consequently avoid unnecessary obstacles. We truly can experience God's best blessings.

## OUR VISION CHANGES

Everyone has a story. And once you have decluttered your own story you will be more mindful of others' experiences and their own unique stories. You will also understand that our story is part of a much bigger story — God's story for all of mankind.

Consequently, rather than criticizing other's behaviors that are not what you hope for or anticipate, you will be able to react differently; rather than rushing to judgment you will allow yourself to be curious. You will be more apt to ponder what their story is and what they have been through that has led them to their behaviors.

I have heard it said that we tend to judge others on their *actions*, but we judge ourselves on our *intentions*. What if we learned to look at everyone's intentions first and gave them (and ourselves) the benefit of the doubt? Certainly that would be beneficial for any relationship!

Also, as you develop a more vibrant relationship with God your eyesight will change — not literally but figuratively. You will be able to seek God's view and ask Him to help you see others as He does.

## PEACE OF A TRANSFORMED LIFE

Ultimately, if we cooperate with Him, God will guide us through a transformation process. The type of transformation that must take place can best be illustrated with the following folktale:

Apparently a woman who was participating in a bible study found herself pondering Malachi 3:3(a). It says, "He will sit as a refiner and purifier of silver." She began to wonder what this meant; how it described the character and nature of God. So she decided to investigate further.

She contacted a silversmith and scheduled a visit to his shop, explaining she simply wanted to learn more about the process of refining silver.

As she watched the silversmith, he held a piece of silver over the fire and let it heat up. He explained that when refining silver, one needs to hold the silver in the middle of the fire where the flames are hottest, in order to burn away all the impurities.

The silversmith went on to say that he had to keep his eyes closely on the silver the whole time it was in the fire. If the silver was left in the flames a moment too long, it would be destroyed.

The woman was silent as she pondered the information. Then she asked the silversmith how he determined when the silver was fully refined. He explained that he knew each piece was finished when he could see his own image in it.

The same can be said for each one of us. Our lives on this earth are all about a transformation so that when others look at us they'll see Jesus; when others interact with *us,* they'll experience *Him.*

Others are always watching how we, as followers of Christ, handle the challenges of daily life — especially challenges that typically cause fear in us. For example, living with an incurable diagnosis like stage four pancreatic cancer.

Thankfully, because my relationship with God is both vibrant and still growing, I have had an incredible sense of calm and quiet joy. I've been very happy *despite* our circumstances — my husband's cancer and my own. I've experienced a deep inner peace that has truly been unshakable.

---

**Philippians 4:7 describes it this way,
"Then you will experience God's peace, which exceeds
anything we can understand. His peace will guard your
hearts and minds as you live in Christ Jesus."**

---

## GREATEST IMPACT

When we maintain a healthy relationship with God, we will find ourselves free of being self-absorbed. That does not mean we ignore ourselves, for we know the importance of maintaining a healthy relationship with ourselves. At the same time, however, we are positioned to seek God's will above our own. As a result, we can be utilized most effectively for His Kingdom purposes.

## THE FOLLOWING MEMORY OF MINE ILLUSTRATES
## THIS PARTICULAR BENEFIT:

One day God gave me a vision where I was standing on the sidewalk along a busy street. He was standing right beside me and had His right arm around my shoulders. We were both looking intently at a high rise building across the street from where we were standing. He asked me, "What do you see?" As I squinted my eyes and looked even closer, I saw a doorman standing in front of the revolving door. I then realized the doorman was Jesus!

At that point God gave me a gentle nudge and together we crossed to the other side of the street. As we approached Him, Jesus smiled and took me by the hand as He led me inside the building. Next He ushered me over to the bank of elevators and pushed the button.

When we stepped into the elevator, I reached for my ID badge. Believing I was not good enough, I figured my room would be in one of the worst locations of the building. At the same time, however, Jesu took out his own ID badge with His credentials displayed on it. He waved it in front of the elevator scanner and as he did He again smiled at me; this time with a bit of a wink as if He had a wonderful surprise for me.

Within just a few minutes we arrived at the top floor. He ushered me out and there we stood — in the foyer of the presidential suite! He showed me around the place, stopping at the door of a particularly beautiful room. Over the doorframe was a plaque with my name on it. Again, he smiled at me and said, "This is the place I've prepared for you. There are floor-to-ceiling windows because my children are meant to be a bright light."

He went on to explain that I had been living with a false identity, and consequently had been hiding my light. Now it was time to claim my true identity and live accordingly, with the confidence to make my biggest impact, all for His glory.

Later God led me to the following scriptures that reinforced the vision He provided for me: Matthew 5:15 says, "No one lights a lamp and then puts it under a basket. Instead, a lamp is placed on a stand, where it gives light to anyone in the house."

Living with a vibrant relationship with God allows us to do what we are created to do; to allow His light to shine brightly in and through us.

## LIVE WHOLEHEARTEDLY

Ultimately, developing and maintaining a personal, vibrant and healthy relationship with our Creator is the only way to live wholeheartedly; living with nothing to fear, nothing to prove, nothing to hide, and nothing to lose. It is the way to enjoy every bit of the freedom that Christ purchased for each one of us. **Nothing else will fulfill the longing in our soul, and that is by God's perfect design.**

---

**Living wholeheartedly means living with nothing to fear, nothing to prove, nothing to hide, and nothing to lose. Matthew 22:37-39 says it this way; love God, yourself and others with ALL your heart.**

---

## LET'S REVIEW THE BENEFITS OF A HEALTHY AND VIBRANT RELATIONSHIP WITH GOD:

- The assurance of spending eternity with God
- Increased joy right now, despite even challenging circumstances; we no longer sweat the small stuff
- Experiencing God's love, which is the greatest love of all
- A change in our vision; we see others with a Kingdom perspective
- Experiencing a transformed life where others recognize Jesus within us
- Having our greatest impact on others, for God's Glory
- Living with the peace, confidence and joy of living wholeheartedly
- Living with nothing to fear, nothing to prove, nothing to hide and nothing to lose

# ENCORE

*Articles for Wholehearted Living*

· · · · · · · · · · ·

## THE GREATEST LOVE OF ALL

One of my favorite singers of all time is Whitney Houston. She had a remarkable voice, and on a recent car ride, I heard one of her biggest hits, "The Greatest Love of All." As I enjoyed singing along, it hit me that the lyrics from that song are the bullseye for living wholeheartedly.

I've found the greatest love of all
Inside of me
The greatest love of all is easy to achieve
Learning to love yourself
It is the greatest love of all

Scripture provides the same message; Matthew 22:39 says, "Love your neighbor as yourself." The inherent assumption is that you do in fact love yourself.

Unfortunately, most of us (especially as women) are our own harshest critic; we're extremely hard on ourselves. Sadly, we fail to offer ourselves the understanding and forgiveness that we so easily offer to others.

If you're a mother, how would you feel if someone criticized your child? I know I'd feel outraged! Have you considered the fact that God feels the same way about you? He's not okay with anyone bashing His beloved daughter. You're the apple of His eye and He created you in His perfect image, exactly as He desired.

**So what will it take for you to learn to love yourself?**

Often, it takes patience and methodically decluttering your relationship with yourself. As you connect with your past experiences and your feelings and beliefs associated with those experiences, you can begin to sort through them. As you do, you can learn to let go of the stuff that's been holding you back and preventing you from living wholeheartedly.

Even better, once you learn to love yourself, you'll be in a position to fully experience the love of God, which is THE greatest love of all. (Psalm 136:26)

• • • • • • • • • • •

## MEGHAN MARKLE'S WEDDING AND WHAT IT CAN MEAN FOR YOU

I've been infatuated with the royal family for decades. I distinctly remember in 1981 getting up at the crack of dawn to watch Lady Diana and Prince Charles' wedding. I thought Lady Diana was gorgeous, and I loved her dress. In fact, two years later, the sleeves of my own wedding dress were made to resemble the voluminous sleeves of her dress.

In 2019, along with several other million people, I watched Meghan Markle and Prince Harry's wedding. Ever since the coverage of their nuptials on May 19th, people have been commenting on Meghan's appearance.

Some say she should have had a more elaborate or fancy dress, believing the one she chose was too simple and plain. Others thought the simplicity was beautiful and classy.

Many people commented on her hair. Some thought it was great, since it reflected her natural and simple beauty. Still others thought it was too casual and that it should have been a more elaborate style for such an important event.

Personally, I thought Meghan looked beautiful; however, I hope that neither my opinion nor anyone else's affects her. I hope she has developed an inner confidence and peace, so she can ignore other peoples' opinions of how she looks.

Sadly, Lady Diana never seemed to find that confidence and peace. Even though she was a remarkably compassionate and beautiful woman, she never saw herself that way. Instead, her unhappiness with herself produced insecurity and anxiety. And unfortunately, her insecurities were greatly magnified by being in the spotlight.

Although it looks promising, it's too soon to say whether Meghan has learned to like who she is or not. But the truth applies to all of us. Until we discover our true identity in Christ, we'll flounder. As a result, we'll be overly critical of ourselves and then look to others for approval.

When you embrace your true identity (the incredible woman that God created in you), you'll be less impacted by the opinions of others; it's like having spiritual Teflon — in which others' comments no longer stick.

Whether you're someone famous who lives in the spotlight, or someone who has a much smaller audience, I hope you come to know the truth: You are fearfully and wonderfully made, and you are God's masterpiece. (Psalm 139:14)

That knowledge is the first step to living wholeheartedly: loving God, yourself and others with all your heart.

· · · · · · · · · · · ·

## HOW A FLOWER CAN HELP YOUR FAITH

Throughout my childhood, I was forced to go to church on a regular basis. I continually put up resistance and, not surprisingly, got nothing out of it. It was simply something we did on Sunday mornings before moving on to the next activity.

It wasn't until decades later, when I was 40 years old, that the spark of my faith was ignited. An acquaintance invited me to hear a speaker at her church and surprisingly, at the last minute, I decided to attend. At the time, I had no idea that doing so would change my life.

It was then, as I was sitting in the church pew that Sunday evening, that I first experienced the presence of the Holy Spirit. I don't remember a word the speaker said, but I could actually feel God's presence — and it was so tangible that it brought me to tears.

Over the next few years, my journey was similar to a flower's, one that is planted in rich, fertile soil and gets regular doses of water, sunshine, and fertilizer. I got involved with a healthy church and was introduced to the Bible and people who shared the love of Christ with me. Consequently, my faith began to grow.

I later participated in several Bible studies, listened to worship music, read dozens of books, and met with a Christian mentor; however, unlike that flower, my faith didn't grow quickly; it was a journey that took 20 years and continues to this day.

I eventually started a women's ministry, Wholehearted Living, wrote three books and two Bible studies. Most important is the fact that I'm more focused on my faith than ever before. I'm thankful for the growth that has occurred, and I look forward to blooming more fully in the future.

• • • • • • • • • • •

## MAKE THE CONNECTION!

A few months ago, my husband received an advanced cancer diagnosis. Just one call turned our lives upside down. The next morning, we awoke to a gray sky and rain. Usually, when I go for my daily walk or run, I take our dog Mabel along with me. However, that day, I knew I needed to exercise, but also to process everything I was thinking and feeling. I also didn't want to have to give her a bath after getting muddy on a rainy day run. Therefore, I decided to leave her at home.

As I began my run, I saw her sitting at the window looking sad about having been left behind. At that moment, denying her needs so that I could take care of my own felt selfish.

And there's the connection: self-care can feel selfish. But before abandoning my own needs, I took this one simple step: I considered my feelings, but also, the facts.

The fact was Mabel would be fine not to run that morning, as she would have other chances for exercise throughout the day. The fact was that I didn't have time to give her a bath before my first appointment of the day, and I desperately needed some time in which to think and pray without interruptions.

When contemplating acts of self-care, think about treating yourself like a good friend. To do so can mean saying "no" to someone or something else (even your pets), so you can say "yes" to taking care of yourself.

Your relationship with yourself is the foundation for all your other relationships; a great way to nurture that relationship, is to make self-care part of your everyday routine.

Ultimately, the only person who needs to approve of your self-care is you. So what are you waiting for? Go take care of yourself.

•••••••••••

## LIVING WHOLEHEARTEDLY WITH AN "INCURABLE" CANCER

We all have a diagnosis that is "incurable;" we've all sinned and deserve the penalty of death. Isn't it interesting that receiving an incurable cancer diagnosis simply gives a name to something we want to avoid or at least "stay in front of" to prolong our life here on earth?

I often wonder if our loved ones who have proceeded us to Heaven might ask us why we're trying so desperately to prolong our time around here. If you are confident in where you're going and believe it will be awesome (what won't be awesome about living for eternity with our Creator, God,) then that should give us peace regardless of any diagnosis.

An incurable diagnosis is a gift in that it reminds us of our complete and utter dependence on God. If you're putting your trust in someone or something else, it'll disappoint you. For only God is completely faithful and 100 percent trustworthy. All else is like sinking sand. Only God is the foundation that will never fail you.

"This type of cancer is not curable." Those are the words no one wants to hear. However, those are the words my husband is now living with. How would you react to hearing such horrific news?

The first thing we did, together, was admit how disappointed we both were; this was not the news we had hoped to hear. The next thing we did was to begin to talk through the information we'd just received and started to come to terms with it.

Then we laughed as we realized we're all living with a diagnosis of "incurable." After all, none of us are getting out of here alive!

• • • • • • • • • • • •

# THE YEAR I TRUSTED GOD TOO MUCH

I've found that when things are going smoothly, it's fairly easy to place my trust in God. Trust, by definition, means to believe in the reliability of someone or something. It requires the acceptance of something as true, sometimes without evidence.

I routinely trust God; I pray regularly, asking for direction according to His plans and His timing. I trust that nothing is a surprise to God, nor a problem for Him.

However, this past year my trust was rocked to the core. Just ten months ago, my husband was diagnosed with stage four pancreatic cancer. We were stunned! His only symptoms were an occasional unsettled stomach and a general feeling of fatigue.

As we pressed the internist for details, we were given little to no hope. Usually a confident, faith-filled woman, I found myself paralyzed with fear, and my ability to trust God seemed to vanish — at least temporarily.

The thought of living without my husband was more than I could imagine. After 34 years of marriage, he has become my rock. At the risk of sounding like the church lady from Saturday Night Live, next to Jesus, he's the one I turn to on a daily basis.

Fortunately, my spiritual journey has led me to a place where I am confident that God's ways are better than our ways; I know that challenges like this often make no sense to us — at least on this side of Heaven. I also know that God remains faithful and trustworthy.

At our first appointment with the oncologist, he cautioned us not to focus on the gravity of the previous reports and instead, said, "We haven't even been up to bat yet." I told him that although I believe in doctors and medicine, I put greater trust in God's ability to heal. I looked the doctor in the eyes and said, "My husband is going to be the next miracle you get to see." I think the doctor was as surprised by my words as I was. Yet as I made that bold declaration, something began to shift within me.

Over the next four to six weeks, God led me to His promises in the Bible, promises to provide strength and (often) healing. Studying the scriptures fanned the flames of my faith. Slowly, I went from hoping that God *could* heal my husband to believing He *would* heal him.

Today, ten months later, I'm thrilled to report that my husband is doing fantastic! The power of prayer has led us to miraculous results: First, a much deeper trust in God and His orchestration of our lives; and second, the improvement of his health.

He's responded exceptionally well to the chemo treatments and to the prayers of hundreds of family and friends. It appears that we're nearing the finish line of this cancer journey, and I trust wholeheartedly that he'll soon be cancer free.

I often imagine meeting God at the entrance to Heaven. My hope is that I hear Him say these words: "Alicia, You trusted me too much." Of course, I don't think those will be the words any of us will hear, for we all have room to develop greater trust in God.

**As we repeatedly put our trust in God, we can experience the peace, the confidence, and the joy, of living wholeheartedly.**

• • • • • • • • • • • •

# IS YOUR MEMORY BAD?

What first comes to mind when you think of a butterfly? Do you envision an insect with colorful wings that flies?

Sure, butterflies are created with the ability to fly, but before they can fly, there's something important they must do. And that's what we often forget.

Although a butterfly starts out in a comfortable cocoon, it can't stay there. To experience flying, a butterfly has to gain strength, and it does so by struggling to break free from the cocoon. If anything interferes with the struggle, the butterfly won't be strong enough to fly.

I believe the same is true for each of us: we too must fight to gain the strength we need to soar.

Much like being in a cocoon, we tend to get comfortable with our circumstances, and then when challenges arise, we often see them as problems. But if we keep the butterfly in mind, we can approach them as opportunities.

Knowing that our challenges can produce the strength we need, we can give thanks for them; we can embrace our challenges with the hope of soaring high. (Romans 5:4)

• • • • • • • • • • •

# THE TURBULENCE AND PEACE OF TWO CANCERS

The Bible says "Then you will experience God's peace, which exceeds anything we can understand. His peace will guard your hearts and minds as you live in Christ Jesus." (Philippians 4:7 NLT)

I've read that verse countless times and even shared it with others, but that was before the challenges we've faced the past eleven months.

In April of last year, my husband received a stage four pancreatic cancer diagnosis. This was a curveball we hadn't seen coming and it felt like a punch in the gut! At the time, we had no idea what was to come.

Over the next 10 months, we dug deep into our faith. Throughout an extended hospital stay, countless tests and procedures, chemotherapies, and a lot of doctor's visits, we prayed with a fervency unlike ever before. We read God's Word and we declared God's healing scriptures over my husband's body. The result was that he began to experience miraculous results.

The doctors were shocked at how well he responded to the oral chemotherapy — all without any nausea, which is in and of itself a miracle because nausea is the number one side effect of these chemo drugs. And just last week, we learned that the tumors have become dormant and, therefore, they're stopping the chemo altogether.

So how do you explain a guy who looks and feels better than he has in 10 years while being on two chemo treatments? You can't — other than God.

Then, just a few weeks ago, I was diagnosed with breast cancer. My first thought was, "Maybe the oncologist can give us a two-for-one special." I'm kidding! But then I began to receive reactions from friends and family. Many said this was too much for anyone to have to endure, and assumed I was mad that both my husband and I were facing cancer at the same time.

The truth is that I'm not mad or sad or afraid. I suppose some might feel those things if they felt this wasn't what they had planned for their lives. But you see, I gave up my life a long time ago; I gave my life to Christ when I became a believer. And over the past 18 years, I've learned that whatever plans I come up with will always pale in comparison to God's plans. I know that He wants nothing but the very best for me in all things.

**I don't believe for a minute that God gave me or my husband cancer, but I have no doubt that He can use it.**

I believe, much like what my husband and I experienced on an airplane recently, in the midst of a storm, that we're experiencing some significant turbulence. But we're confident we can ride this out and eventually rise above it.

Hence, this is my prayer: "Father, use every bit of this experience; use it to draw others to know You and love You so that when they face turbulence in their own lives, they too, can experience the peace that surpasses all understanding."

Experience the joy of living wholeheartedly!

• • • • • • • • • • •

# HOW TO AVOID AN EMOTIONAL WRECK

We have all been advised to check our blind spots when driving a car. To be a good driver, we have been taught to look for anything that might be approaching and yet hidden from our view.

When it comes to our emotional life we also have blind spots. We all have areas of our lives that can cause trouble, yet we fail to see them from our current position.

**If we fail to look for our blind spots, we'll eventually get into a wreck — physically and emotionally.**

It seems so simple, but when is the last time you intentionally looked at your emotional blind spots? Does the thought of doing so scare you? Are you afraid of what you might see?

Two great resources for recognizing our blind spots are God's Word and a life coach or counselor — both can help us to see what we cannot see on our own.

If you understand that God loves you and wants nothing but the very best for you, it will be more comfortable asking Him to show you the areas in your life that need some attention. Then, understanding that God disciplines those He loves, you can more easily deal with what is revealed to you without guilt or shame.

You can go to His Word and allow it (the Bible)to act as a mirror, reflecting areas in your life that are not in alignment with God's will. It does not mean you will not encounter some challenges along the way, but it can help you to see things differently, and, therefore, avoid unnecessary damage.

When dealing with blind spots, working with a life coach can also be extremely beneficial. Talking through things like your hurts, hang-ups and humiliations can promote smoother travel; you can move forward in your relationships with fewer bumps in the road.

Simply said, if you want to avoid a wreck, deal with your blind spots to-day; seek wisdom from God and a trusted life coach or counselor. (James 1:5 NIV, 2nd Timothy 3:16-17)

• • • • • • • • • • •

# THE ONE THING THAT CAN PREVENT YOU FROM BLOOMING

It is finally spring and that means a variety of flowers are starting to bloom. If flowers are planted in rich soil, receive adequate sunshine and plenty of water, they'll undoubtedly grow and eventually bloom.

But what if a flower was planted in contaminated soil and received very little water or sunshine? What then? Obviously, it would not grow and fully bloom as it was intended.

In that case it is easy to see that the problem is not with the flower, but rather with the lack of nourishment and other unmet needs.

Unfortunately, many women are just like that flower — they did not receive what they needed to grow and thrive. They did not receive the emotional, physical and spiritual support that every child needs. Conse-quently, they have failed to bloom and have come to believe they are the problem.

That is so unfortunate because that is simply not true. What's worse, the belief they are flawed or somehow not good enough can cause them to focus on others' needs and ignore their own.

If this rings true for you, there is good news: it is never too late to see that your needs are met — that you get everything it takes to grow and thrive.

See that your roots are planted deep in the soil of God's love for you; get plenty of Living Water (God's Words) and provide the sunshine of grace, supportive affirmations and encouragement. Eventually, your energy and confidence will soar and you will be able to celebrate the incredible wom-an in you, in full bloom!

• • • • • • • • • • •

# HOW TO GET RID OF UNWANTED GUESTS

When you hear the phrase "unwanted guests," what comes first to your mind? Do you think of bugs and other critters that would require an exterminator? Or instead do you think of some relatives that come more often than you would like or stay longer than you would prefer?

The type of unwanted guests I have in mind are the ones who damage your home — not your physical home, but your emotional home. For example, there is the guest who enters your home and proceeds to hurl accusations at you and remind you of all your past mistakes. She would be called guilt.

What about the one who insults you, pointing out all the things you are not doing well and reminding you that you should be doing better? She would be called the critic. In addition, you've probably encountered the one who gets to the core, reminding you that who you are is not enough — not pretty enough, not smart enough, not successful enough. She would be called shame.

The obvious question is why would you let people like that into your home? Why would you spend time with them? Of course, I am not talking about real people here, but rather, parts of us that live within ourselves.

Unfortunately these unwanted guests seem to sneak in without your awareness. The longer they stay the more confident they become, and, consequently, the more damaging their behaviors.

Over time, the presence of unwanted guests damages the relationship with yourself. Since that relationship is the foundation for all your other relationships, it affects everything. The situation might sound helpless, but fortunately it is not. With some very simple steps you can eliminate those unwanted guests and restore your home.

First, remind yourself that you are no longer a helpless child. Today, you are a mature adult with the ability to make wise choices. Make the decision and follow through. Tell the unwanted guests (in no uncertain terms) that they are to leave and leave now! You might even consider writing an eviction note to them. It might sound a bit dramatic, but I assure you it can be extremely empowering.

The second step is to extend an invitation to the guests you enjoy. Invite those who are helpful and encouraging, those who love and support you. Also, welcome those who speak the truth in love, who hold you accountable and yet affirm you. Open your arms wide to those types of guests and allow them to stay indefinitely.

As you learn to live with guests whom you wisely choose, you will experience a healthy, vibrant and fulfilling relationship with yourself.

• • • • • • • • • • • •

# HAVE YOU OVERLOOKED THIS PRIVILEGE?

God's Word tells us that we are to run the race of life and to do so with perseverance. Unfortunately, we can carry heavy burdens, and those burdens can leave us exhausted and overwhelmed.

Hebrews 12:1 provides the answer to our woes; it says that we are to strip off every weight that slows us down. God is well aware that we have been lugging a backpack full of bricks that makes our journey much more tiring that it needs to be. And because He loves us, He wants to help us lighten our load.

To live the life God has prepared for us we need to declutter. To run the race well we need to get rid of the physical, emotional and spiritual stuff that weighs us down.

**Clutter is simply the accumulation of failures — in particular, failing to make a decision.**

If we fail to make decisions about our material possessions, they will quickly accumulate. When taken to an extreme, you could find yourself paying for extra storage units! The truth is that too much physical stuff can cause stress and trouble that no one needs.

When we fail to make decisions about our emotional stuff, we hurt others, we prevent the healthy and fulfilling relationships we crave and we withhold our best, which is a loss for everyone.

When we fail to make decisions about our spiritual stuff, we suffer the most devastating consequences of all; our spiritual clutter causes distance between ourselves and God.

The good news is that with the help of a coach you can declutter your life. If you do, you will be amazed at how great you can feel and what you can do. In fact, with less stuff you can experience the peace, confidence and joy of living wholeheartedly!

• • • • • • • • • • • •

# THE SECRET YOUR POSTURE REVEALS

Recently, while preparing for an upcoming speaking engagement, I asked God to provide a picture to me — a picture of what it means to live whole-heartedly. He soon brought to my mind a distance runner participating in a relay race.

After praying for clarity about the vision, the connection became crystal clear.

To be a successful relay runner one must have the right posture. She must be able to reach forward to grab a hold of the baton and reach backward to release it.

To live wholeheartedly you must have a similar approach; you must look ahead and behind. Look forward to those from whom you can learn.

Learning requires a posture of humility; you must recognize the fact that despite all your experience you do not know it all. That acknowledge-ment is not to make you feel bad, but instead to promote a desire to learn from others with the right attitude.

In addition to reaching forward you must also reach behind; you must reach back and lend a hand to someone who has not yet covered the ground that you have already traveled. Who might benefit from what you have learned and experienced along the way?

To live wholeheartedly, you must learn to give and receive; in other words, maintain the posture of a relay runner. (2nd Corinthians 9:6-7, Matthew 22:37-39)

Start today. Ask God to show you whose hand you are to reach for and who is reaching for your hand.

• • • • • • • • • • •

# A LIFE THAT COULD IMPACT YOUR OWN: CHARLIE CUTLER

You likely do not know Charlie Cutler, but I was fortunate enough to have known this handsome and vibrant young man, if only from a distance.

My husband and I have been blessed to be friends with his parents, Chuck and Diane, for more than 30 years. During that time, they raised four incredible young men: John, Scott, Peter and Charlie.

Because our kids were different ages and went to different schools, we did not know their boys very well. However, their youngest son, Charlie, impacted my life in ways I could not have imagined.

In 2012, Charlie was finishing his last year of college at Iowa State University where he subsequently received his bachelor's degree in architecture. During that spring semester Charlie was diagnosed with, not one, but two types of Non-Hodgkin's lymphoma.

Over the next three years, Charlie was in and out of numerous hospitals. Too many doctors, surgeries, tests, appointments and heartaches to mention. What always struck me was his unrivaled optimism and joy no matter what he was enduring.

It wasn't that Charlie just faced an occasional setback; he faced monumental, devastating setbacks, over and over and over again. Yet despite the circumstances he faced, the light of his effervescent personality never dimmed.

On the bulletin board above Charlie's hospital bed, they kept a sign that read, "When you choose hope anything is possible." And that is exactly what Charlie did every day of his life.

On March 10th of 2016 Charlie passed away. Days later, my husband and I attended the ceremony to celebrate Charlie's life. As we were hearing about the tremendous impact Charlie had on his family, friends and so many others, I had a crystal-clear vision. In it, I saw Heaven welcoming Charlie home with the same overwhelming joy of a maternity ward that welcomes a new baby.

I believe that somewhere deep inside us we all hope for the same; we want to have made a meaningful impact on those we leave behind and to receive a warm welcome to Heaven.

Whether dealing with current health issues or just the challenges of everyday life, I often reflect on Charlie's approach to life and his commitment to choose hope.

God's Word says, "May the God of hope fill you with all joy and peace as you trust in Him, so that you may overflow with hope by the power of the Holy Spirit." (Romans 15:13)

Regardless of your current challenges, may you come to know the hope of God's only Son. Then your hope can overflow and impact others, like Charlie's did.

A new program was established at John Stoddard Cancer Center (in honor of Charlie) that seeks to empower cancer patients and caregivers to maintain a high quality of life and provide the tools to live each day fully. It's named the Charlie Cutler Healing and Wellness Program.

The program recognizes that a cancer journey involves more than just traditional medical treatments. Cancer is a mind, body and spirit experience. Integrative therapies offered by this new program, such as massage therapy, aromatherapy, guided imagery, acupuncture, meditation, yoga etc are proven to strengthen patients and help both patients and caregivers live each day to its fullest potential.

Here's where you can find out more about the Charlie Cutler Healing and Wellness Endowment: https://www.unitypoint.org/desmoines/comfort-therapies.aspx

# DO YOU HAVE YOUR FATHER'S EYES?

Who do you look like? Whom do others say you most closely resemble? Do you often hear that you look just like your mother? Or maybe, like me, you hear, "You certainly have your dad's blue eyes."

Not only did I inherit my dad's blue eyes, but I also inherited some of his personality traits and interests. What about you? When it comes to your words and actions, to whom are you closely related? Do you have the drive of your father or a great sense of humor like your mother? Maybe you build things like your dad or pay attention to the details like your mom?

Regardless of which relative you resemble or act like, we can all grow in our resemblance to Jesus. More specifically, we can learn to see with a Kingdom perspective. This is important as our ability to see with that type of perspective will help us to live wholeheartedly.

So what kind of perspective do you have when you look at yourself? How do you see yourself? Are you hyper-critical, believing you are not good enough or that you are insignificant? Or do you take the Kingdom perspective that God does?

When God looks at you He sees a beautiful, talented and incredible woman. He sees the life of impact He has designed for you and how your story is part of a bigger story. The challenge then, is to see ourselves and examine our lives through His eyes — confident that we are more than what we currently think we are and are equipped for things we have yet to imagine.

Not only must we learn to see ourselves as God does, but also, we must see others as He does. Putting that Kingdom perspective to work when examining others means that, rather than rushing to judgment about people, we can be patient and demonstrate compassion for them; we can remember they too have a story. Similarly, when others see obstacles in their way, we can help them to see God's provision for them.

In 1979 Amy Grant recorded a song called "Father's Eyes" that quickly became a favorite of mine. The lyrics provide words for this Biblical approach:

> When people look inside my life, I want to hear them say:
> She's got her Father's eyes, her Father's eyes
> Eyes that find the good in things, when good is not around
> Eyes that find the source of help, when help just can't be found
> Eyes full of compassion, seeing every pain
> Knowin' what you're going through, and feeling it the same...

Maybe the best compliment any one of us can receive is, "You have your Father's eyes."

• • • • • • • • • • • •

# BELIEF OR UNBELIEF? WHICH IS IT?

A cancer journey starts out with a shock. In 2017 my husband's diagnosis of stage 4 pancreatic cancer was a curve ball we had not seen coming. Initially, we were scared, confused, overwhelmed and anxious.

With some time to sort through our thoughts and feelings, however, we eventually settled back into our normal. We were able to focus on our faith and trust that God would provide everything we needed.

For the most part, his cancer has not affected our daily quality of life. My husband still works full time, goes to the gym several days a week, does our yard work and even does most of our cooking — all the normal things he did prior to having cancer.

However, this week we head back to Mayo Clinic for some important test results.

Especially today, I am reminded of something important that I have learned in this process: I have learned to hold two conflicting thoughts or beliefs at the same time.

In other words, while I DO believe, I also pray for God to help me with my unbelief.

I continually teach about the importance of validating our thoughts and feelings, and so I have told myself I have every reason to feel a bit anxious about the results.

AND, at the same time, I focus on what I believe with every cell of my body: God loves my husband and He wants nothing but the very best for him, ALWAYS. I believe God will provide complete healing in His timing and as He knows is best.

That is how we have had inner peace, confidence and joy — regardless of any doctor's visits, test results, or anything else. That is what it means to live wholeheartedly.

If you are struggling with belief and unbelief (or any other conflicting beliefs) give yourself permission to acknowledge both.

**Lord, I believe; help my unbelief. (Mark 9:24)**

# AFTER PARTY

*Questions for Discussion,*

*Reflection and Growth*

The following questions can be processed alone or with a group. However, a strong word of caution: If you choose to dive deep with others in a small group, I would do everything you possibly can to promote and maintain a safe, confidential setting. That is crucial so participants can share their deepest feelings, thoughts, wants and needs. It's only when we're willing to be vulnerable with one another, that we can truly experience deep, heart-felt connections — and in the end, that's what we all crave.

It's also helpful to draft a simple contract or some guidelines to clearly address confidentiality and commitment to attend the discussion or study sessions. In the absence of establishing that up front (and having everyone who participates agree to abide by them), you'll inevitably run into problems; rather than helping women get free from their hurts, you'll potentially hurt them in the process of sharing.

I'd also suggest starting and ending the group sessions with prayer; acknowledging the presence of the Holy Spirit and asking God to provide a safe, confidential opportunity for each participant to feel heard, understood, respected and loved — all while leading us to greater knowledge and intimacy with Him.

It can be a tremendous opportunity for growth for the individual participants, if you rotate and have everyone take a turn opening and closing at least one of the group sessions with prayer.

• • • • • • • • • • •

# ACT 3: YOUR RELATIONSHIP WITH YOURSELF

## YOUR UPBRINGING:

1. While reviewing your upbringing, how do you explain the concept of not choosing a side?
   a. How can you honor your parents and be a fan to yourself?
   b. At first thought, who are you more inclined to protect — your parent(s) or yourself, and why?

2. Big or small, what are one or two of your favorite memories from growing up?

3. What are one or two of your least favorite, or most hurtful or challenging memories of growing up?
   a. If you could go back to those situations, what would you want to tell yourself?
   b. What might you be waiting to hear to be able to move forward with peace about those situations?

4. If the story of your life was documented in a book, in what genre would it be classified: Comedy, Drama, Action Adventure, etc.?

5. What were some great qualities that you inherited from your mother and/or father? How are you thankful and appreciative of the things your parents provided for you — emotionally, physically, financially and spiritually?

6. How might your relationship with your father be contributing to your less than desirable treatment of yourself?
   a. If you could go back and talk with your dad, and be honest about your unmet needs, what might you want to say?
   b. If that were to happen, how would that impact your ability to move forward and leave that emotional baggage behind? Might there be someone else that's even more important to helping you get free to move forward (like yourself)? What might that look like; what would you need to tell yourself?

7. How might your relationship with your mother be contributing to your less than desirable treatment of yourself?
   a. If you could go back and give a message to your mother (about your unmet needs) what would you want to say?
   b. If that were to happen, how would that impact your ability to move forward and leave that emotional baggage behind? Might there be someone else that's even more important to helping you get free to move forward (like yourself)? What might that look like; what would you need to tell yourself?

8. Did anything traumatic or unsettling happen in your childhood that you weren't allowed to talk about and work through your thoughts and feelings? Was something swept under the rug and ignored?
   a. What are you afraid of? What makes you hesitate to bring the situation out into the light?
   b. If so, what emotional price will you continue to pay if you keep hiding that experience?

9. Knowing we all make mistakes, how have you dealt with shame or guilt from your past?
   a. What emotions have you attached to the story you've been telling yourself about the experiences that produced shame or guilt?
   b. If one of your good friends was involved in the same situation, how would you likely respond with grace and compassion?
   c. What would it look like to be a fan to yourself, and to treat yourself as a best friend — specifically in regard to those experiences?
   d. What do you think Jesus would want you to do with the shame or guilt from those experiences?

**YOUR PRESENT:**

1. How would you describe the concept of becoming your own fan, rather than one of your harshest critics?
   a. Do you have some beliefs that could cause resistance to the idea of treating yourself as you do a best friend or neighbor?
   b. What parts of yourself do you have trouble loving or valuing? What do you dislike or view as "not good enough"?
   c. According to Jesus' words in Matthew 22:37-39, what is the implication about your relationship with yourself?

2. What feelings are hardest for you to identify or admit?
   a. Do you allow yourself to get mad or sad?
   b. Do you give yourself permission to be frustrated, stressed or discouraged?

3. Do you have others with whom you feel safe enough to share anything you may be feeling or thinking?
   a. If not, what's preventing you from investing in one or two women to develop that type of relationship?
   b. Who might God have put in your life that might be that good friend in which to develop a trusted, supportive relationship?
   c. Who might need you to be that supportive, safe, confidential listening ear?

4. In what areas are you most critical or hard on yourself?
   a. Can you identify where or when those critical thoughts or behaviors got their start? (In your past, from other relationships, etc.?)
   b. Do you have unrealistic expectations of yourself and if so, where might those have gained their start?

5. In what specific areas or relationships do you find the most resistance to being your own fan?
   a. At work or with acquaintances? With friends or family members?
   b. In what relationships are you experiencing a lack of peace; where do you often experience anger, frustration, disappointment, sadness or fear?
   c. What is the message of Proverbs 4:23?
   d. What is the message of Matthew 22:39

6. What are one or two of the toughest things you've gone through in your past, that you could now use to help encourage others who might be dealing with something similar?

7. How do you handle mistakes that you make? Do you find you're defensive? What about your reaction when receiving constructive criticism?

8. In what areas of your life are you most inclined to make comparisons?
   a. How do those comparisons make you feel?

   b. What quality would allow you to be freer of the tendency to look to others to make comparisons?

9. When you review your current schedule, do you feel that you're busy or overscheduled a bit?
   a. When you find yourself over committed how do you "numb out"?
   b. What beliefs cause resistance to you establishing and maintaining healthy boundaries?
   c. How would it feel to have a schedule in which you are truly invested in what you've committed to be part of, and to include regular times of rest and relaxation to get restored?
   d. What prevents you from establishing that type of a schedule?

10. What are the deepest concerns of your heart this week?
   a. What is the narrative you've been telling yourself about those concerns?
   b. How can you take those concerns to God?
   c. What are your beliefs about God's approach to handling those concerns of yours?
   d. How might you get assistance from others to handle those concerns?

• • • • • • • • • • •

# ACT 4: YOUR RELATIONSHIP WITH GOD

**YOUR UPBRINGING:**

1. When (at what age) and how were you introduced to having a faith?

2. How did your faith make you feel? Sinful, safe, scared, protected, etc.?

3. How did your parents and other family members model the principles of a Christian life?
   a. Did they attend church, pray at mealtimes, serve others in need, etc.?
   b. Did they make your own spiritual development a priority? If so, how did they do that?
   c. Did any of their words or behaviors seem inconsistent with what you believed it meant to live as a Christian?
   d. Did they regularly study the Bible?

e. Did your parents ever take a huge leap of faith? If so, what did that involve and how did it turn out?

4. If you could go back and change something about your spiritual upbringing, what might that be, and why?

5. Looking back at your upbringing, even if your parents didn't acknowledge it at the time, do you feel like God's Presence and provision were evident?

## YOUR PRESENT:

1. What are you most common thoughts about your relationship with God?
   a. What three words would you use to describe God?
   b. How do you think God feels about you? And what is your proof to back that up?
   c. What do you think God expects or wants from you? Again, what is your source to back that up?

2. Do you often feel distant from God? And if so, what do you sense is causing some resistance to connecting wholeheartedly with Him?

3. How do you most deeply connect with God? Through music, tradition, nature, studying His Word, hearing sermons, reading devotionals, etc?

4. What are some of your prayers that God has answered in significant ways in your life?

5. How would you describe your approach to prayer?
   a. How comfortable are you with praying to God?
   b. Do you regularly focus on asking for your needs or those of others?
   c. Do you regularly give thanks and show appreciation for what God has done in your life?
   d. How do you feel about sharing with God the seemingly insignificant, small things that are concerning you?
   e. How do you think God feels about your prayer life, and your prayers?

    f.  What is the message of Hebrews 13:15-17 NLT?

6.  Have you had experiences where you believe you've heard from God?
    a.  In what way have you felt direction from God?

7.  Are there particular scriptures that you feel have been especially important to you in your spiritual journey?
    a.  If so what are those verses and why are they meaningful to you?

8.  What talents, skills and experiences are you utilizing to help others?
    a.  Are there unique talents, skills or experiences that you undervalue and believe aren't exceptional or good enough to be helpful to others?
    b.  What beliefs might be causing resistance to you stepping out and utilizing your talents, skills and experiences for the Kingdom's benefit and for God's glory?

9.  Are you familiar with the types of spiritual gifts?
    a.  What are some of the spiritual gifts that are included in the 8th chapter of Romans?
    b.  How is love connected to the use of our spiritual gifts?
    c.  Do you know your own spiritual gifts? If so, what are your thoughts about your spiritual gifts?
    d.  Where or how are you using your spiritual gifts and talents at his point in your life?

10.  What are the most common people or things that cause distractions from focusing on God and your relationship with Him?

11.  What is your current approach to the Bible?
    a.  Do you regularly make time to read God's Word?
    b.  Do you utilize Bible study groups or other ways to deepen your understanding and application of God's Words?

12.  Do you think it's important to regularly attend a church or worship service, and why or why not?

13.  Do you regularly make rest a priority or do you routinely run yourself ragged until you're burned out or sick?
    a.  What prevents you from resting?

b. Do you routinely honor a Sabbath rest? Why or why not?
c. What is the message of the following scriptures?
    i.   Genesis 2:3
    ii.  Exodus 20:8-11
    iii. Leviticus 23:3
    iv.  Deuteronomy 5:12-15
    v.   Ezekiel 20:19-20
    vi.  Isaiah 58:13-14
    vii. Matthew 12:12
    viii.Mark 2:23-28
    ix.  Luke 13:10-17
    x.   Hebrews 4:9-11

14. If you could grow in one particular area of your relationship with God, what would that be?
    a. What might be resources or places you could encourage growth in that area?
    b. How would you feel about seeking out a spiritual mentor or someone who has a greater knowledge of Scripture and/or a deeper faith that could help provide guidance and encouragement for your own growth?

• • • • • • • • • • •

# ENCORE:

## THE GREATEST LOVE OF ALL

1.  In your own words how would you state the message of Psalm 136:26?

2.  What things prevent you from loving yourself exactly as you are?
    a. What things about your upbringing cause resistance to believing you are lovable or worthy of being cherished?
    b. What current things provide resistance to loving yourself?

3.  How do you typically handle a genuine compliment about your appearance or something you've done?
    a. If you resist a genuine compliment how do you think that makes the person feel that gave you that compliment?

b. What causes you to resist a compliment; what prevents you from simply accepting it and saying, "thank you"?

## MEGHAN MARKLE'S WEDDING AND WHAT IT CAN MEAN FOR YOU

1. If you were in the media spotlight, like Meghan is, what do you think you'd struggle with the most?

2. In this article, what is the key to learning to like yourself?

3. In what areas do you find other's opinions matter significantly to you?

4. Can you think of an example where someone else's opinion swayed your own opinion — whether for good or for bad?

5. What is the message of Psalm 139:14?

## HOW A FLOWER CAN HELP YOUR FAITH

1. Was church a part of your upbringing?

2. What about prayer; was that done on a regular basis, occasionally or never at all?

3. In what ways was your faith encouraged or enhanced in your young adult years?

4. Who were two or three people who had a positive impact on the development of your faith?

5. Did anyone have a negative impact on the development of your faith?

6. Have you had the opportunity to be a person of influence on another's development of faith? If so, please share about that experience. If not, how might you seek that type of opportunity?

## MAKE THE CONNECTION

1. What is the false message we're given about self-care?

2. What is the truth about self-care?

3. In what ways do you make self-care a lifestyle? Please provide two or three specific examples.

4. What is an example of something that might be considered self-care to one woman but not to another?

## LIVING WHOLEHEARTEDLY WITH AN INCURABLE CANCER

1. How does it feel to think about the fact that we're all living with an incurable diagnosis?

2. How do you think you'd react if you or a loved one received a diagnosis of an incurable cancer?

3. What might be your first concerns or fears?

4. To whom or what do you look to for security?

5. How would you describe what it means to live wholeheartedly with an incurable cancer or other catastrophic diagnosis?

## THE YEAR I TRUSTED GOD TOO MUCH

1. In hindsight, what challenges have you survived that you later saw some good that came from them?

2. What is the message of James 1:2-5 NLT?

3. In what areas do you struggle to trust God completely?

4. What beliefs promote your resistance to putting your trust completely in God?

5. What can "fan the flames" of your faith; what can encourage growth in your faith?

6. On a scale of 1 to 10, how much of a priority is the development of your faith? And would your schedule/calendar reveal that to be true or not?

## IS YOUR MEMORY BAD?

1. From what challenges did you gain strength to soar — emotionally or spiritually?

2. How comfortable have you gotten with your comfort zone?

3. How do you feel about God nudging you to step out of your comfort zone or to take a leap of faith?

4. What thoughts or beliefs cause resistance to trusting and following God where He is leading you?

5. What is the message of Romans 5:1-5 NLT?

## THE TURBULENCE AND PEACE OF TWO CANCERS

1. Share an example where you experienced an unusual sense of peace in the midst of a significant challenge?

2. What was the source of your peace?

3. Was your peace evident to others who were close to you?

4. Share an example of a turbulent time in your life that caused you to struggle to find God's peace. If you could go back to yourself at that time, what would you now want to tell yourself? What did you learn from that turbulence?

5. What is the message of Philippians 4:7 NLT?

6. What are the potential benefits of facing and surviving difficult challenges:
   a. For yourself?
   b. For other people?

## HOW TO AVOID AN EMOTIONAL WRECK

1. What are two good sources to help you identify your blind spots?

2. Over the past year or so, how have your blind spots caused problems for you or others who are close to you?

3. What are some good resources to help you gain clarity about your blind spots?

4. What is the message of James 1:5 NLT?

5. What is the message of 2nd Timothy 3:16-17 NLT?

## THE ONE THING THAT CAN PREVENT YOU FROM BLOOMING

1. Was your upbringing equivalent of a healthy start; were you planted in good rich soil, watered often and received the sunshine needed to develop a growing and vibrant relationship with Jesus?

2. Has anyone given you a particularly meaningful book, CD or other resource that was a catalyst for your faith to grow?

3. What or who provides encouragement for your spiritual growth at this point in your faith journey?

4. How might you help to nourish another person's development of faith?

## HOW TO GET RID OF UNWANTED GUESTS

1. How often do you feel that you're hard on yourself?

2. Who are "helpful guests" that are affirming and encouraging for you?

3. How might you be a better guest for yourself every day?

4. Who is an "unwanted guest" that you could be conscious of leaving outside your front door?

5. What is the message of Proverbs 4:23 NLT?

6. What is the message of Luke 10:27 NLT?

## HAVE YOU OVERLOOKED THIS PRIVILEGE?

1. What is the message of Hebrews 12:1 NLT?

2. What do you think is your biggest source of clutter; what is the heaviest baggage you continue to carry with you?

3. What physical clutter could you make decisions to eliminate or reduce?

4. What emotional clutter would be beneficial to get rid of?

5. Is there spiritual clutter that's causing resistance to a more vibrant, fulfilling relationship with God?

## THE SECRET YOUR POSTURE REVEALS

1. Whose hand are you reaching for to encourage spiritual growth?

2. To whom are you extending your own hand, to help them with their spiritual growth?

3. What are ways we can help one another to develop a healthier, more meaningful relationship with God?

4. What is the message of 2nd Corinthians 9:6-7 NLT?

5. How would you define living wholeheartedly?

## A LIFE THAT COULD IMPACT YOUR OWN

1. What is a really difficult challenge you've face in the past?

2. During that time what was your source of your hope?

3. What is the message of Romans 15:13 NLT?

4. What type of impact do you hope to leave as your legacy?

## DO YOU HAVE YOUR FATHER'S EYES?

1. What qualities did you inherit from your earthly father?

2. What three words would you use to describe your earthly father?

3. What three words would you use to describe your Heavenly Father?

4. How do you think your relationship with your own father impact your approach to your relationship with your Heavenly Father?

5. Who is someone in your life that you feel you struggle to see through God's eyes? To whom do you struggle to love, like, or to give the benefit of the doubt?

6. Who is someone in your life that you see through God's eyes even if others do not?

## BELIEF OR UNBELIEF? WHICH IS IT?

1. In what areas do you find it fairly easy to believe and trust that God will provide exactly what you need?

2. In what areas of your life do you struggle the most with unbelief?

3. Do you think that admitting areas of unbelief is a sign of weakness or strength, and why?

4. What is an example of a topic or situation in which you currently hold two seemingly conflicting beliefs?
   a. How do those conflicting thoughts or beliefs make you feel?
   b. What benefit do you see in holding on to each of those conflicting beliefs?
   c. How might you share those concerns or beliefs with God and seek His truth about them?
   d. What benefit might there be if you were to find a peaceful resolution to those conflicting thoughts/beliefs?
   e. What is the message of 2nd Corinthians 2:5 NLT? And what does that mean in your own words?

# ABOUT THE AUTHOR

*Alicia Economos*

Alicia Economos lives in Des Moines, Iowa, with her husband Ted and their dog, Mabel. In addition to their daughter, son and daughter-in-law, they spend their time hosting and laughing alongside a large network of relatives in their big Greek family.

Alicia enjoys speaking, coaching and connecting wholeheartedly with others. Whether in person or online, her enthusiasm and faith-filled optimism are obvious from the moment you meet her. She likes yoga, running and reading, and is passionate about helping women develop healthy relationships with themselves, with God, and with others.

Alicia is the founder and director of Wholehearted Living; a program that helps women declutter their lives (emotionally, physically, and spiritually) so they can make their greatest impact and live their best life.

• • • • • • • • • • •

## FAN MAIL

If you found Alicia's story helpful or meaningful to you, please feel free to share your comments with her at info@aliciaeconomos.com or connect through Facebook or Instagram (alicia.economos)

• • • • • • • • • • •

## SPEAKING

In addition to being an author and a certified life coach for the Wholehearted Living program, Alicia Economos is a highly sought-after speaker.

Drawing from 20 years of coaching, Alicia shares the simple steps to develop more fulfilling relationships: with God, yourself and others.

With a fast-paced, interactive and often humorous approach, she shares personal stories you will relate to. Hearing about her own decluttering journey, you can't help but be inspired to get rid of your own clutter (the stuff that weighs you down and prevents you from living wholeheartedly).

Alicia also provides the simple tools that have helped hundreds of others to live their best life, that you can immediately put to use in your own life. Although she speaks primarily about living wholeheartedly, she also speaks on a variety of other topics and will happily tailor her message to address the desired outcome of your event or the needs of your audience.

## HERE'S WHAT OTHERS HAVE TO SAY ABOUT ALICIA

"Alicia's passion to help others comes through in her presentations. She is an amazing speaker, keeping her audience engaged and sitting on the edge of their chairs." — *Dr. Tyler Molstre, Wellness Doctor at True Life Wellness*

"Words to describe Alicia include authentic, heartfelt, passionate, delightful, enthusiastic and faithful. She is an excellent speaker, writer and heart coach. Alicia is a WOW!" — *Lynn Heggen, Independent Health, Wellness & Spiritual Director*

## HIRE ALICIA

To hire Alicia to speak at a future event or to conduct a workshop for women in your community, please visit her website aliciaeconomos.com or contact her at info@aliciaeconomos.com.

# OTHER PRODUCTIONS

*by Alicia Economos*

. . . . . . . . . . . .

## BOOKS IN THE WHOLEHEARTED LIVING PROGRAM

1. Your Relationship with Yourself — Learning to love and like who you really are

2. Your Relationship with Cravings — Living in harmony with food, your body, possessions and more

3. Your Relationship with God — Learning to love God with ALL your heart

# REFERENCES

Chandler, Steve. Seventeen Lies That Are Holding You Back and The Truth That Will Set You Free. California: Renaissance Books 2000.

Economos, Alicia. Your Relationship with God, Learning to love God with all your heart. Kentucky: Create Space 2012.

Economos, Alicia. Your Relationship with Yourself, learning to like who you really are. Kentucky: Create Space 2012.

Eldredge, John & Staci. Captivating, Unveiling The Mystery of a Woman's Soul. Tennessee: Thomas Nelson 2010.

Nelson, Mary J. JEHOVAH RAPHA, the God who heals: Barbour Publishing, Inc. 2016.

Rothschild, Jennifer. Self Talk, Soul Talk. Oregon: Harvest House Publishers 2007.